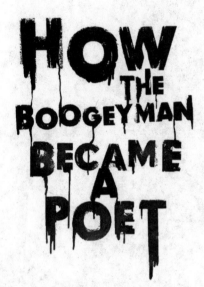

HOW THE BOOGEYMAN BECAME A POET

TONY KEITH JR.

 KATHERINE TEGEN BOOKS

An Imprint of HarperCollins Publishers

Katherine Tegen Books is an imprint of HarperCollins Publishers.

How the Boogeyman Became a Poet
Copyright © 2024 by Tony Keith Jr.
Photographs courtesy of Tony Keith Jr.

Library of Congress Control Number: 2023936873
ISBN 978-0-06-329600-8

Typography by David Curtis
23 24 25 26 27 LBC 5 4 3 2 1
First Edition

Take no one's word for anything, including mine, but trust your experience. Know whence you came. If you know whence you came, there is really no limit to where you can go.
—James Baldwin, *"A Letter to My Nephew,"*
The Progressive Magazine *(1962)*

This is for all of my nephews.

Love,
Uncle Tony

SPRING 1999

I CAME OUT IN THE WORLD LIKE "THIS":

bright and burning,
a brilliant little Black star,
weighing every bit of seven pounds, seven ounces, measuring
    nineteen and a half inches long.
        cesarean cut right through Ma's center,
           smack-dab in the middle of hot July   on the
                seventeenth day   in the year 1981.

I was carefully carved fresh from her flesh at a hospital on a
    military base in Freehold, NJ,
where Pop was training to be an airman basic.
        same way, same place, same space where my sister Tamu was
           born just seventeen months before.

my whole body arrived on fire,
flaming from the warmth of my mother's womb.
medical records say I was an infant prone to ear infections that
    raised my internal temperature well beyond a boiling fever.
I was three when I bubbled over 102.7 degrees Fahrenheit.
made me tug at my lobes a little too hard for Ma's comfort,
doctors put some tubes in there to help cool down the noise.

3

they fell out a few months later while I was dancing circles
    around my shadow.
        wound up scarring some tissue on one of my eardrums.
        now I be tripping on vertigo.
            it's like the world be spinning around if I climb
                far too high   and try
            to look too straight up toward the sky,
            or stare too deep down beneath the earth's belly.

I was in eighth grade when the flames brought me scarlet fever.
spread these sensitive-ass bloodred bumps across my entire body,
causing some pain to rise up in the middle of my chest.
        emergency room doctors said Ma brought me in just a few
            moments before
        the infection punched its way into the second layer of my
            beating heart.

legend has it, my being here was a close call too.
apparently, Ma, twenty-three, pregnant (unplanned) with me,
drove a four-door powder gray Dodge Diplomat   with tires that
    foolishly assumed
the tread on their rubber wheels was deep enough to skate slick
on smooth black ice   during cold winter.
        round rubber dummies didn't test themselves first: CRASH!

Me and Ma: us: we slid like lava on concrete water.
her belly becomes an inflated safety airbag bracing all my
    bouncing.
we both survive unscathed,

4

save for the twenty-three railroad track stitches Ma had stapled
    across her forehead.

I remain submerged,
                baked golden brown,
birthed by scalding summer.

Ma always tells the story of our accident whenever she's explaining
    to other people
why I am   *the way I am*.
her "baby": funny, curious, clever, smiling, singing, dancing,
    joyful, carefree, bright, showy,
a ball of colorful energy, making life fun for us all.
she'll say to them, while looking at me,
"*something* must've happened to him, because that boy ain't been
    right since."
and then she'll chuckle with a sweet laugh that don't hurt.

unlike last year, when I turned sixteen,
and Pop echoed Ma's tale with a gallon of sour sugar
that still stings me in some place I don't yet have the language for.

for real for real,
I'm far too afraid to discover what *it* might actually mean,
because whenever I think about what my father *actually* said,
the Boogeyman creeps out from some dark corner of my bedroom
    closet
and I can't get any sleep at night.

POP HAD JUST GOTTEN OUT OF REHAB AGAIN.

he called to wish me happy birthday.
after confirming that I was indeed being a good boy by reading
    my Bible (I was not),
and praying for my salvation every day (I was not), he goes,

<blockquote>
"First Corinthians 2:9 says,
eyes have not seen,
nor ears have heard,
nor has it entered the heart of man
the things which God has prepared for you.

I'm proud of you, son,
but as a baby, you cried so daggone much
I thought you were gonna grow up to be a
'sissy' or 'something'"
</blockquote>

as if, "something" disguised what he *actually* said.
as if, there was probable cause for concern about my safety.
as if, I am not mirror to his namesake.
as if, there was reason to question my capacity
to survive an attack from the source of saline

I tasted on tears dripping from the tip of my tiny toddler tongue.
as if, my center was too vulnerable,
and so, I had to curl up into myself for comfort.
as if, all my screaming and hollering
triggered some insecurity *he* had about *my* density.
as if, there was a layer of flesh and spirit
I left lingering inside of Ma fifteen summers ago.
as if, no tissue is attached to vein, blood, bone, muscle, fat, or skin,
and therefore, I was too soft and too sticky
to withstand whatever hard stuff Black men must make light of
in order to feel strong enough
to hold on to and hold up themselves.
as if, there was trivial possibility of my power
to protect my own peace during times of war.
as if, I entered my physical existence with an unarmed and
untrained military
that was ill-equipped and unprepared
to battle beasts that prey on the bodies of little Black boys
who are unafraid to express how they *really* feel on the inside.

AND LET MY PARENTS TELL IT,

I came out curious before crying.
a queer kid full of questions,
complete with some kind of "knowledge" embedded inside the
    brain
holding up my big-ass Black head.

I had a curved ledge attached to the back of my skull
that Pop, former jock, would wrap his hands around and hold
    like a football
before pretending to launch me into the air,
and I'd swirl around the atmosphere, giggling at my father's
    gentle touch.

Ma tried smoothing out my knowledge mountain with her
    soft hands:
    same ones she used to grease Pop's hair as a teenager
    and twirl batons between her majorette fingers at their
        homecoming parades
she mushed and mashed what I came out knowing into a
    more manageable size
until my body grew into itself.

my parents called the back of my head a "puck."
I've no idea why they chose this word,
as there was never a time in our lives *together* when hockey was a
    part of any discussion.
as a kid, I only knew a puck to be:

      some black round thing that skates smooth on slick ice,
      and that people on two sides of a thing with razor blade feet
         and long curved sticks
      love to beat around until the puck submits
      to being captured in a net disguised as a protected space for
         its safety.

      and this happens so much
      that it's only a matter of time before one side is crowned
         victor,
      and the puck is exposed for all that it really is:

      a piece of black property destined to be locked and stacked up
      inside of a cage, in the dark, with the rest of the pucks
      and all their knowledge.

      until the next game time, when they will again
      inspire some fight about them between people on two sides
         of the thing,
      who will be cloaked in armor,
      and will ignore how badly the puck's been beaten,

and how naked and cold it's been for what feels like centuries.

until some black-/white-striped/skinned person with
    authority
blows a whistle before the brawl begins.

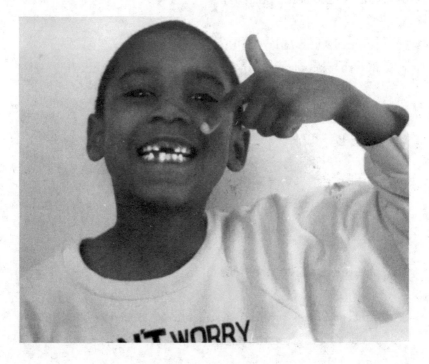

MY KNOWLEDGE OF SELF:

the history of who I am
explains how I came to be a seventeen-year-old senior at DuVal
   High
where our mascot, the Bengal tiger, is the largest living cat species
although I can barely stretch my body out from beyond this
five-foot, four-inch brown border.

DuVal High swallows a corner block of a busy intersection in
   Lanham, MD,
in Prince Georges County (PG)—green land partially circling
   around the first-ring suburbs
of the diamond-shaped District of Columbia (DC).

for real for real, I don't think I'm built like most of the other Black
   boys here.
I weigh in at about 120 lbs. soaking wet, with all my clothes on.

I don't feel like my shoulders are strong enough to stand on,
nor can I puff my chest out enough to appear as large as I believe
   I am.

Ma keeps saying I should be enrolled in a "weight *on* program,"
with a chuckle, that sings a different tune
now that she's shopping at department stores specializing in
     clothes for plus-size women.

word is, I was a baby who couldn't drink directly from my
     mother's breast,
nor could I stomach processed milk that was squeezed from some
     strange cow's udders,
so, liquefied soybeans were my sole source of survival
until I could chew and swallow solid foods without needing any
     synthetic assistance.
now, the doctor says my calcium is too low
and that's apparently why my fingernails, which I can't stop
     chewing around,
got all these dark brown lines streaking their ways across them.

and that's why, in seventh grade, my dentist told Ma that my state
     of smiling
would eventually need some "straightening out."

I entered high school in 1995,
as a thin-ass Black boy with crooked teeth barred up in stainless
     steel wires
and colored rubber bands that my mother's medical insurance
     didn't cover.
     got them taken off junior year.
          now every tooth is finally sitting still in its right row,
          shining from its own designated space inside my mouth.

accidently dropped my expensive-ass retainer in a trash
	can at McDonald's
we can't afford to pay for another one.
		now, my bottom jaw is starting to stretch out
			farther than the top one does.

my face can't decide on what shade of its own natural color
these acne spots should show up as,
I am sweet-and-stale-skinned chocolate chip cookie Black boy in
	the mirror.

plus, my vision got blurry sophomore year,
had to join the rest of my family in wearing prescription
	eyeglasses.
		so, I can't tell what I *really* look like while peering through
			medicated lenses
		that layer over all the things I don't always love about myself.

and ain't enough bass and treble flowing through the sound waves
	of my weak voice.
I can't thump hard enough to vibrate skyscrapers
I can't create a strong cocoon around myself
to feel secure about my safety when I'm around certain boys.

I never speak up when I know that some of them be speaking
	down to me.
		those slick and sly, shy moments when they'll quietly slither
			the word "soft"
		out of their sneaky, greasy mouths.

or they'll call me "weak," as a way to describe my peculiarly small
    size,
        my significantly troubling short stature.
            this always causes me to question my own strength.

to be clear, I've been called "skinny" by a whole lotta different
    people,
most of whom, I know, love me,
like Ma, who also says I am the way that I am because I eat like a
    bird.
        truth is, I think my appetite for Ma's cooking and my anxiety
            about being bullied
        be throwing hip-hop parties together in the basement of my
            stomach,
            setting the roof on fire.
                they never ask for water either.
                they just prefer to let me burn, burn, burn.
I don't be that hungry, for real for real.

I've also been called a "bitch" and a "punk" and a "pussy" and a
    "faggot"
far more than a few times over the years to ignore
how often I see the Boogeyman lurking around some of these boys
    at DuVal High.

THE ATHLETIC PLAYGROUND BULLY BOYS,

the ones I try to avoid, like Tahron,
who, in fifth grade, picked me last to be on his basketball team at
    recess:

he was a popular tawny giant with quick and aggressive moves
and all of us knew that he hogged the ball longer than anyone else
    should,
yet none of us ever questioned his power to do so.

I was surprised on the first play of the game
when he passed me the bumpy orange rock and yelled out,
"don't fuck this up, Tony!"
                    I blink. I catch. I stop breathing.
no one taught me how to play basketball
nor what rules to follow and so,
with both hands palm-pressed against this golden sphere of
    masculinity,
I bounced the thing on the ground,
pivoting my whole body toward the hoop
and stepped out on both my left and right feet.

"double dribble!" cut through the air and sliced my wobbling legs
    in half.
I tripped over myself and fell to my knees
landed on my back and rolled on my right side
        the blacktop rubbed a thin burn on my elbow.
the impact didn't hurt as much as seeing everyone else
pointing their fingers directly at my sad little brown face,
laughing at how "funny" of a man I was going to be.

to make matters worse, Tahron shadowed over my shine
and screamed into my soul, "what the hell was that, Tony?!
you can't do stupid shit like that!
go sit your *gay* ass down somewhere!"
then, he pushed both of his fists into my chest
using a force lighter than gravity   disrupting my
    equilibrium
and so I fall again,
only this time, I land on my butt and slide backward across the
    gravel,
tearing more holes in my gently used wardrobe.

"stop it, Tahron!" screamed out Chavon,
one of my classmates who I think also knew something about
    playground bullies.
she ran over to me with her long arms extended
                            publicly acknowledging my humanity,
and with her sweet hands,   helped hoist me back up vertically.
I could only look at the stitches loosening across the top of my
    off-brand sneakers

as I sequestered myself to sit on the sidelines where all the girls
    were   safe(r).

I didn't cry on the outside
as I watched some of those girls cheer for their favorite playground
    bully boyfriends
        the ones who told me:
            I got a caged-bird chest made of bouncy rubber
           and butterfingers attached to the ends of my flimsy bent
                wrist.
                    they say these are the reasons why I can't catch,
                    pitch, or run for shit.

I SAVE MY TEARS TO CRY LATER

on the pages, where the poems go:

they just be falling on me sometimes
like comet-sized hailstones bopping me upside my noggin,
ancestral asteroids
knocking rhythmic words into my noodle.

my poetry be descending at lightning speed from,
I guess, some place in the solar system where
telescopes and astronauts only see swirly sparkling black holes.

whole time, it be all my unwanted emotions
and all my sensitive-ass questions in there
running around in opposite directions
on a cosmic racetrack made out of concentric circles.

and because they don't always show signs of arrival,
I write them down on whatever paper
and with whatever pen or pencil or marker
that is within radius of the crater created from the blast.

I was thirteen when the first poem burst in my atmosphere like
    dat,
disrupted my window-seat view of the mountaintops on high,
while riding in the back seat of Pop's Jeep
headed south to Knoxville, TN, where his father (Pop-Pop) is
    from.

I was sad, and I don't remember why,
but I know that I wanted to cry,
but I ain't want anyone to notice,
so, I wrote a poem on a tiny notepad that I kept in my backpack
    trying to get to the root of the feeling.
I watched the ink make wells to catch tears that couldn't fall:

HOUSE ON THE HILL

look at the mountains outlining the sky
they shine with a glow so beautiful
that it blinds the eye

in the middle of this scene
sits a little white house up on a hill
it holds the grass and the trees
its old looks keep it still

inside is unknown
could be an old man, a ghost
or maybe emptiness

its wooden off-white steps
are rubbed by weather
a broken chimney leaves it helpless
a place where a window once sat
and maybe where a person viewed out

now, it looks abandoned
and dead

you can hear its loneliness shout

why is this house up on a hill?
so alone and so still?
what's inside?
what keeps it standing?
goes without knowing

Look at the mountains outline the sky
They shine with a glow so beautiful
that it blinds the eye
In the middle of this scene sits
a little white house upon a hill
It holds the grass and the trees
Its old looks keeps it still
Inside, is unknown could be a   or maybe
old man, nothing a ghost or emptiness
emptyness
It s has wooden off white steps
robbed by weather and a broken
chimney leans it helpless
A place where a window once sat
and maybe a person viewed out
Now it looks abandoned and dead
You can hear its loneliness shout.
Why is this house up on hill so
alone and so still
whats inside and what keeps it
standing goes without knoledge

LOTS OF FOLKS KNOW I WRITE POETRY

it's no secret in my family that I have a "thing" with words,
and most of my friends at DuVal High know I'm the man with the
    poems,
but they only know me for the birthday poems
and the one-month puppy love anniversary poems,
and the cheer my sad friend up on their worst day poems,
and the happy father's day poems they give to their mothers on the
    third Sunday in June.

in fact, Ms. Peralta, our senior-class advisor,
asked me to share a poem dedicated to the Class of 1999
during our senior-year talent show next month.
I'm not sure what I'm gonna write about yet,
but I believe the universe will fling something from its innards
that will land somewhere behind my eye socket.

at least, that's what I told my girlfriend Blu on the phone last night
while we were watching *Love Jones* together on HBO.
        we began as day-one best friends in eighth grade at Goddard
            Middle School,
        where I met my other two "girl-friends": Tiffy and Ebby.

I was always the only boy in their sisterhood fellowship
circle.

"remember when we first saw this at the movies?" Blu asked.
"yup, that's when you forced me to hold your hand underneath my
jacket!" I said,
laughing a hole in my throat.

        I heard the blush flowing into her rosy cheek.
        I bet she was smiling as hard as I was.

"if I recall correctly, I didn't have to force you, Mr.,
in fact, it was *you* who slid your warm fingers through mine first,
talking about how cold it was in there," she said, sucking through
her teeth.

        Blu is right, I did make the first move.
      there is something about the way Darius Lovehall
        commands the audience
   with a standing microphone, African drums, and a jazz band,
    and describes his first encounter with Nina Mosley
        through a metaphor
       as the blues in her left thigh
     that was tryna become the funk in her right
    that made me feel like us touching in private *like that*
      was absolutely alright, alright, alright.
     I want to move a crowd like that too someday.

Blu said I should perform one of the love poems I wrote for her at the talent show.

I be writing ones that cause her to bat her eyelashes like fluttering
   butterfly wings:

a reaction and a reflection that always fills me up.

like this one, that ain't got no title, but she enjoys the rhyme:

UNTITLED

silence has many sounds
laughter is full of pain
a heartbeat doesn't pound
sunshine has rain
you speak with no tongue
you see with no eyes
one plus one is one
there is truth in all lies
you can hear with no ears
you can feel with no hands
there is courage in fear
there is water in sand
what goes up doesn't come down.
the moon shines during the day
there is a sky on solid ground.
and there is snow in May.
raindrops never fall.
the desert is not dry.
you can walk through brick wall.
tears don't come from eyes.
there are many things that will never be true
that is except for *me* and *you*.

Silence has many sounds
laughter is full of pain
A heart beat doesn't pound
Sunshine has rain
You speak with no tonge
You see with no eyes
One plus one is one
There is truth in all lies
You can hear with no ears
You feel with no hands
There is courage in fear
There is water in sand
what goes up doesn't come down
The moon shines during the day
There is a sky on solid ground
And there is snow in May
Rain drops never fall
The desert is not dry
You can walk through a brick wall
Tears don't come from eyes
There are many things that will never be true
That is except for me and you

my heart, my private parts, and my poems
be playing mind tricks the moment my pen scratches the paper.
I want all of what Blu and I got beating inside of our chests,
and I yearn to dance to the rhythm beating through our bones,
but I can't deny my curiosity about the boys
that also causes my body to go thump thump thump.

I write love poetry to her, and for her, and with her,
because she is a safe audience for my most secret and sacred pieces:
 the ones describing my real dreams and desires to be in love,
 and to be loved,
  all while burning, flaming, and on fire.
   when *those* poems stretch out from the sun's surface,
    I feel brighter than the darkness that keeps me up
     at night.

when I write *those* emotions deep into the page like *that,*
and Blu responds the way she does: recognizing who I am beneath
 the words,
she reflects a beaming light that blinds the Boogeyman from my
 sight,
and I feel like I have feathers large enough to fan myself into the
 wind.

I WRITE FOR SAFETY,

I need literal protection from boys like Tahron,
the ones who've developed grown-man muscles mutating underneath
   their thick skin.
and I've seen some of them in the weight room pumping around
   impossible pounds of iron.
huffing and puffing and lifting and lunging and squatting and
   curling and pulling.

           I'm sure some of them could bench-press me up and down
                                        if they wanted to.
                                  if I wanted them to.
                        I think I want them to.
              I think some of them want me to, too?

this is why I don't play any sports at DuVal High.
nor do I layer up in athletic wear on weekends to defend
the front or side lines of some neighborhood team
full of rough and tough Black boys who tackle each other and
   don't shed any tears.

I do not stick around after school to hit jump shots just for

"fun"—it never is.
street rules ain't regulated like refereed games in our school gym.

plus, some of the ones that pat each other's butt as a physical
    reward for teamship,
        as an intimate celebration of athletic achievement,
also believe that a "pat on the butt" ain't always *just a pat on the
    butt*.
it all depends on whose hands are at play,
whose backsides are on display,
which one of them looks "some kinda way,"

                                    which one of them is gay . . .

and the ones who are suspect of being too curvy to walk the flat line
                    become the rear end of jokes about boys and butts.
but the bottom line is,
I don't want to be pushed to the ground again.
I don't want my backside scarred up from sharp blacktop pebbles
all because of some great misunderstanding about my wrong way
for naturally bouncing basketballs around with my bare hands
and the way I slide swiftly on my size 8 feet,
and that any of that has to do with the people I wanna get busy
    with.

they don't know that Blu and I been discovering what it feels like
to be close enough for our bodies to touch the outer and inner
    layers of our skin,
and to kiss each other on our lips and in our mouths,

and on our necks and underneath our shirts sometimes.

plus, I've had several girlfriends before.
truth is, I started kissing girls with my tongue in third grade,
back when my friend Travis dared me to do to Jelani
what Steve Urkel did to Myra on *Family Matters*.
I went all the way to second base in seventh grade
after Dhalia asked if I wanted to taste what her boobs looked like.

I enjoyed those moments too:
all that tension buzzing through me and
not being sure what to do about it
except press play on the TV shows and movies
in my imagination.

and besides, everyone knows that Blu and I have a short-distance
   relationship.
     she transferred from DuVal High to Bowie High at the
       beginning of sophomore year.
I assume this truth is why I have not been the brunt of any bully's
   inquiries
about my "straight" performance.

I NAVIGATE THROUGH SCHOOL AS SAFELY AS POSSIBLE.

DuVal High is a mix of Black and brown students and like five
    white kids.
there are quite a few adults in the building who look like me,
although I somehow end up in classrooms taught by most of the
    white ones.
one of them is Mr. Marshall,
a ginormous man with baby powder skin, sapphire blue eyes,
and balding, cranberry-orange hair.
his voice always seems to sustain a tone slightly above a whisper,
but never louder than his breathing will allow.

he teaches psychology, advises our student government association
    (SGA)
and is a walking dictionary full of fancifully large and long words.
he'll casually blurt some of them out in class sometimes
    midsentence
as if we all know what the hell he be talking about.
I always ask him for the spelling and definition of the ones that
    fascinate me most.
I write them down in my blue spiral notebook.

I feel like one day, I'm gonna need to know what these words
    mean.
as if, preparing early for some time in the foreseeable future
when I will need to confront some battle of wits,
which can't be fought with bare knuckles and closed fists
and I'll have no other choice
but to draw on the strength of my vocabulary
and push the power of words out of my mouth whenever I spit.

I learned this lesson when I ain't win my seventh-grade spelling bee.
the word I had to spell was "clavichord."
confident in my ability to spell words the way they sound in my
    head,
and not really knowing what the hell some of them mean,
I run one hundred miles an hour from my seat
and make a hard stop two seconds before almost falling into Ms.
    Lyte's desk.
            she is one finger on one handful of my Black teachers.

Ms. Lyte's classroom becomes a stage.
I approach the mic, take a deep breath, and smile extra hard
    underneath my braces,
and then recite each and every letter clearly: "C L A V I C O R D."
"I'm sorry, Tony, that is incorrect," Ms. Lyte says,
in a tone that sounds like honey but feels like disappointment.
she continues, "Karen, you're up next."

before I could muster up enough emotional energy

to logically prove why my spelling was indeed correct,
this little white girl named Karen,
> who sat in my same row, just two columns down on my left,
> and who *always* had something to say,
walks right into *my* moving spotlight.
and with a smile that is too sweet for my taste,
she announces with authority: "C L A V I C H O R D."
Ms. Lyte goes, "that is correct, you'll be representing our class in
> the semifinals!"
then she politely slams truth into my face: "Tony, you were super
> close!"

I smile from inside and start walking one mile an hour back to my
> desk.
that's when Karen decides to inform me   in her outside voice
(when she really could've just whispered the shit)
that the letter "h" I missed in the spelling of "clavichord" is rooted
> in its
Greek/German/Polish origins.
apparently, a clavichord is a sixteenth-century medieval stringed
> instrument,
which has something to do with European history,
and for real for real, that's just not a subject I find particularly
> interesting.

I smile at little Karen without parting my lips,
nod my head down   and then back up again,
and say, "thanks for letting me know."

whole time, I was tryna figure out how she knew something
about the English language that I didn't,
and whatever that thing was, is the thing
that boosted her up higher above me in the spelling bee.

this is why I'm taking Latin this semester with Mr. Johannsen
he says there are no known living native speakers of the language.
     so, I am learning something dead
that is helping me break words down into their b a r e b o n e s
     b a s i c b i t s
before deciphering their definitions.

DETERMINING THEIR DERIVATIVES.

the word Mr. Marshall gave me yesterday was "diatribe,"
a forceful and bitter verbal attack against someone or something.

I wonder if my AP English teacher, Ms. Nyland,
is gonna go on another one of her diatribes today.
it's almost lunchtime and so far, she ain't felt compelled to tell me
that I need to:
enunciate my words more "clearly,"
"articulate" myself better,
make sure my subjects and verbs always agree,
regardless of whether or not the American
standard
ever agrees with me.

Ms. Nyland says that I can't drag my dirty language all over the
filthy ground
and expect to speak squeaky clean on paper.
especially if I want any chances of getting accepted to college.
some academic feat that no one in my family has yet to
complete.
Tamu graduated from DuVal High last year and enrolled in a

computer tech school,

and everyone else in our family went straight to working
government jobs.

although ain't nobody pressuring me to be the first in my generation
to do so,

I'm just excited about the possibility of it all.

it doesn't help that, based on our standardized test scores,

DuVal High has a reputation as one of the "lowest performing"
schools in PG,

so, it's not too many names listed on the alumni college acceptance
board

that's been stapled to the main office door for the last five years.

so, what do I know?

and what can I say to Ms. Nyland:

this blond-haired, blue-eyed, middle-aged white woman
who has already called Ma twice this year to explain how
disruptive I am in her class.

apparently, I talk too much and I talk back to her too much too.

but I be telling Ma that Ms. Nyland be the one starting the shit.

like that one time when she asked me to tell her what line and
page number from:

The Scarlet Letter / The Crucible
Crime and Punishment / Brave New World
The Iliad / The Odyssey / Romeo and Juliet

when some unfamiliar character did something that I didn't care
about,

and she requested that my response be followed up with
a critical analysis of the context in which these classic tales were
     constructed
by all those crusty old, and coffin dead, white men.

                         so yes, I told her to stop acting like a "jerk."
            and yes, I called Ms. Esterbaum "senile" in fourth grade
                  because she ain't let me finish sharpening my pencil
                                             on the wall thingy.
and yes, I also informed my fifth-grade teacher, Ms. Longfellow,
                  that she was a gigantic smelly rotting butthole
        after kicking me off a class field trip before the bus departed
                  because I forgot to bring my permission slip.
     and yes, I asked Ms. Schneider to kindly "kiss my Black ass"
                                             in sixth grade
                  only because she told the whole class
                  that I don't read instructions clearly
     and yes, I instructed Mr. Roberto to "shut up and go to hell . . ."

it's just that all those white teachers were talking down/at/through
     me in a way
that I felt   was far too comfortable for them.
     they remind me of my playground bullies.
     they remind me that I feel angry, often.
     they remind me that I'm sad, sometimes.
     they remind me that I'm constantly confused about my world
          changing.
          they never asked me to write, read, or speak about any of
          that.

Ma is right though, it was not right   or just of me
to purposely use words as weapons
with intentions to inflict harm on people's feelings

                              even if they hurt you.

so, I always apologized the next day.

ENGLISH CAN BE SCARY SOMETIMES.

hands down, my favorite classmate at DuVal High is Tolu:
4.0 GPA every quarter, former class president,
competitively ranked track and field athlete, current student body
    president
she's destined to be valedictorian at graduation.
her family is Nigerian, and yesterday at lunch,
while dreaming out loud about college life,
Tolu told me underneath her signature strong smile
that her family plays absolutely "no games" when it comes to their
    education.
she said her parents did not come to America
just for her or her sisters to bring shame upon their ancestral
    names.

                    whole time, I wish I knew my ancestral African name.
        I should ask Ms. Nyland if she can critically contextualize *that*,
                            but Ma might get another phone call.

I love watching how tediously Tolu takes notes on everything she
    reads
and just about anything Ms. Nyland says,

structuring every word neatly into sentences that are perfectly
        situated on the blue lines
of the white paper stitched together inside of her violet spiral
    notebook.
        her knowledge system seems far more sophisticated than the
            scribble scrabble
        chicken scratch of scholarly words I sloppily record in Mr.
            Marshall's class.

Ms. Nyland has instructed us to pair up with a partner
and compare notes that we were supposed to take on the reading
        of a critique
about Fyodor Dostoevsky's literary works.
I read it, but didn't understand any of it,
so I look over at Tolu ready to absorb her wisdom,
and instead of digging into nineteenth-century Russian literature,
    she asks,
"did you finish your personal statement, Tony?"

                                                        nope.

I take a deep sigh and then, I lie,
"uh, yeah, I've got most of it done, just gotta finish up the
    conclusion,"
she responds, "alright, let me know if you need help,
now is not the time to get distracted.
remember, our success is a journey, not a destination."
        Tolu is so wise.

I don't tell her that I am retaking the SAT tomorrow morning,

or that when I took it last October, all I got was an 850 out of
    1600,
and when I took it again this past February, I flatlined with a
    score of 920.

I don't tell her that although I have a cumulative 3.75 GPA,
and was sergeant of arms for SGA junior year,
and was in AFJROTC my sophomore year,
Ms. Nyland says all my extracurriculars ain't gonna suffice.
        she says I need *at least* 1200 points to compete with other
            "high achieving" students.
and I ain't studied nary a thing out of the thick-ass book she gave
    us this semester
that's supposed to teach us the tricks to making confident guesses
about the best and right answers on this stupid-ass exam.

for real for real, all of it looks just as wrong as Ms. Nyland is about
how right   I know   my writing is.
she always tryna tell me that my essays are missing their theses,
and that my arguments are disorganized and unsupported,
and that while my attempts to write creatively are wonderful,
this class ain't about the literary arts,
it's about critical analysis and composition.

but she don't know dat I be penning poems in the margins
                        when she ain't looking through my joy.
            when she ain't tryna snatch the voice out my throat.
                when she ain't scrunch-faced annoyed about me
                    as if, historically, I did something to her

that she doesn't remember,
neither can she explain,
but she is certain that I'm the person responsible
for why she's miserable teaching this classroom
full of talented and gifted Black children.

each one of us tagged: selectively chosen to run on an academic
track
in a lane that ain't supposed to have no hurdles
taller than our high GPAs will allow us to jump over.
I may have a sharp way with my words,
but I ain't never failed a class or gotten a grade below a B before.
I intend to keep it that way.
with Tolu's help and by conceding to the standard, I've got an A in
this class,
but I ain't taking the AP exam because I know my score won't win
me any college credits.

Anthony Keith, Jr.
AFJROTC 10; Modeling
Club 11; SGA 11; Class
Olympics 11
I plan to get a degree in
business management and
start my own business.

I HATE FEELING LIKE DIS,

all incapable of greatness and unwilling to waver from some
   purpose,
but also believing that some things are, indeed, impossible,
   like this class.
I wonder if Tolu actually cares about any of this shit,
or if she's doing her own performance too.
perhaps Ms. Nyland only sees this as some theatrical production
that she ain't want to be a part of in the first place,
but Principal Burns forced her to play the role of our teacher.

                        maybe we're all sick and tired and angry
                  about all this acting we're doing on the world's stage.

my greatest spectator as of late has been the Boogeyman.
and I'm trying to focus on what Tolu is saying about socialism and
   suffering
but I'm wondering how long It's been standing there   *this time.*
   It never announces Itself.
   It don't say nothing either.
It just stares at me through the window of our classroom door
speaking some kind of spell under Its tongue,

forcing me to talk differently than how I think.

cuz I be thinking 'bout "dis"
and end up sayin' "that"
and then I'll say "this"
when I really mean "dat"
and den, I mean "then"
when I think of "dem"
I end up saying "them"

my speech gets all twisted and confused with my writing
   sometimes.
feels like I'm constantly tryna decipher some code
to balance the weight of words dat be coming out my brain,
wif da words dat be fallin'

out

of

my

mouf.

as if there is some kind of Black version of English
embedded somewhere inside the African American parts of my
   pink tongue.

for real for real, I've been wanting to know more about Africa
   since sophomore year,
when, for Black History Month,
we took a school-wide field trip to the movies to watch *Amistad*.

I'm vexed afterward, thinking about all those free African
    folks
fighting with those colonial white folks
on a slave ship leaving Cuba headed toward America.
and Cinqué shouting out, "give us, us free!"

and I'm wondering if perhaps,
I should lead some sort of revolt on the bus ride back to
    DuVal High
because all of us Black kids have stuff to say
about what we just saw on the big screen
and none of our chaperones care to discuss any of this
    with us.

now, I got all these questions about my ancestors:
            the ones who survived all that mess
            so that Ma and Pop could make me.
            curious of their stories about freedom
                floating around inside of my head
                restricted.

I don't tell Tolu none of dis,
I just lower my head to focus on her cedar eyes
instead of the classroom door,
where the Boogeyman's face is pressed against the glass,
pointing Its pin-tight pupils directly at me.
and I nod my head in agreement when she volunteers to be our
    group's spokesperson

and says a bunch of brilliant words about Dostoevsky's philosophy
   of God and love.

whole time, I'm thinking about something else:

FIRST TIME THE BOOGEYMAN CAME FOR ME.

it all started when I became Black at six years old.
I was running around a church with some cousins on Pop's side.
we knew there was a tiny window of time left before service began,
so, all of us are sans shoes, sliding on our socks, pants creased,
    shirts half-tucked,
ties unclipped, wings extended, flying in between pews,
being lightning bolts of busy-bodied Black boys.

until an elder, vexed, screamed from outer space
with a baritone belting up from his gut, "sit your <u>Black</u> behinds
    down!"
we pause hard and shift our gaze toward his furrowed brow and
    slanted lower lip
and awaited further instructions.
with a tongue laced in both love and fear, he proceeds,
"as long as you're 'Black,' you better *not never* get caught barefoot
    in public!"

confused and afraid, we all flipped our smiles
then stuffed our sweaty feet inside of plastic hard
burgundy and brown penny loafers (with actual pennies)

and placed our hind parts on a row of purple padded seats
where the Martin Luther King Jr. fans are tucked away
just as tightly as our joy.

the elder did not explain *why* what we were doing was wrong,
nor was he specific about what would happen to us if we got
    caught again,
but I sensed in his voice that "being Black" was something
    negatively associated
with the presence and movement of my body.

although, I doubt that our child's play disrupted
whatever guilt adults went to church to pray about,
but certainly our behavior,   and our skin,
represented some borderline between innocence and sin.

I remember sitting there   silent
while my brain screamed questions out loud like:
        what is it about my speed and feet that make me a target
        for some supernatural force tryna restrict my movement?

    how do I make myself appear smaller, softer, lighter, and quieter,
        when all I want to do is be big, loud, fast, and free?

will I have to forever filter out parts of myself that draw too much
                                    attention
        from something I don't even have the language to name?

what will happen if I am captured?

will I no longer be Black?

and if I am not Black, then what will I become?

I lay awake in bed that night with my comforter covering me from
   the nostrils down,
staring at a dark spot standing tall and still in the corner next to
   my dresser.
I hadn't seen that thing before.
      not sure where "It" came from, but that glob of dark energy
      knew me well enough to know how terrified I was to confront
      It.

normally, Ma played the Quiet Storm mix on 96.3 WHUR with
   DJ Melvin Lindsey,
and I'd drift off to dreamland slow rocking myself to the sounds
   of:
Sade / Atlantic Starr / Stacy Lattisaw / Phyllis Hyman /
Anita Baker / Luther Vandross / Zapp / Keith Sweat,
but that evening, he was in that radio station spinning "Moments
   in Love" by Art of Noise,
which I swear sounds like the scary-ass theme music to *Friday the
   13th* with Jason Voorhees
(not *Halloween* with Michael Myers).

I kept looking at my door, next to the bedroom my parents *used* to
   sleep in together,
      it was cracked open.

Tamu was sleeping in her room down the hall.
I debated about screaming loud enough to grab either of their
    attention
while also outrunning the thing,
but I was frozen flat to my mattress.
my head would not lift off the pillow,
nor could I extend my feet from beneath the sheets to expose a
    single toe.
and I was pretty sure there was something else lurking underneath
    my bed.
I told myself, "remember Tony, the Boogeyman is after your
    Blackness,
so, shut your mouth and don't make any swift movements."

suddenly, It started slow dancing with Its shadow
and without pulling the handle,
slid Itself through a tiny crevice between my wall and the door
    frame,
and took up permanent residency in my closet.

I BE HAVING NIGHTMARES AND DAYDREAMS.

the bell rings and Ms. Nyland, looking relieved, dismisses us for
    lunch.
I, too, am taking a deep sigh of relief because I avoided the
    Boogeyman   for now.
I toss up the peace sign to Tolu and make a beeline for the
    cafeteria,
making sure to avoid hallways where some of the playground bully
    boys be buzzing.
I don't see It in the hallway,
but just in case, I've got the poem I wrote in Ms. Nyland's class
    last week
tucked in my backpack, armed and ready:

    she was busy spewing all her blah blah blahs and womp
        womp womps
        felt like time was moving slower than the few seconds
            before a snail sneezes
    and I was once again thinking about my African ancestors,
    and what time meant for them.
    suddenly, It flashed Its face in the glass square at the top
        center of the door.

I thought it was a passing shadow until I locked eyes on It:
all too familiar and absolutely incorrect.

I didn't make any sudden movements.
I just pretended to follow Tolu's notetaking tactics
but instead of writing words about reading and speaking at
    the college level,
I wrote a poem about what was really going on,
and somehow, that made the Boogeyman temporarily
    disappear:

KILL THE CLOCK

hours stick
the clock ticks
seconds fly in rings
the clock sings
minutes nonstop
the clock tocks
tick tick like awaiting death
ticking away at every breath
annoying at first
and murder soon
down with the sun
up with the moon

it still holds time
it never speaks
but the words rhyme
I wish had the power
to end this hour
it will end for a moment
only to start and tick again

kill the clock

while you sleep
you dream the song
the clock plays all night long
if it's not a tick
it's the click
it's possessed by a demon
that's my reason
it rings each hour
except midnight
but 12:01 it's back in sight
kill the clock

it has eyes
and waits for you to look
then it opens
and reads like a book
it anticipates your mind
wondering the time
and keeps you hungry for more
and ticks
just as loud the stroke of four

kill the clock

Kill the clock

Hours ~~stick~~ stick
The clock ~~tickle~~ ticks
~~Seco~~ Seconds fly in rings
The clock sings
Minutes non stop
The clock tocks
Tick tick like ~~a clock~~ awaiting death
Ticking away at every breath
Annoying ~~at~~ at first
And murder soon
~~Upside~~ Down with the sun
Up with the moon
It still holds time
It never ~~whispers~~ speaks
But the words rhyme
I wish I had the power
to end this hour   it will end ~~x~~ ~~xxxxx~~
~~Stop~~ for a ~~second peace to~~ moment ~~brief~~ ~~xxxxx~~
Only to ~~stop~~ start and tick again
~~Kill~~ the clock
~~xxxxxxxxxx~~ ~~Every sunrise xxxxx~~

THE CAFETERIA IS BUMPING.

I walk inside, looking toward the windows
where I usually sit with my two best boy-friends: Bubba and
    Cubby.
I ain't never scared to be around them.
we've been the best of friends since fifth grade
and are three members of a larger group of Black and brown boys
that hang out in Cubby's basement after school and on weekends.
we call ourselves "The Dungeon Family."
we be playing video games and cracking jokes about each other's
    bad breath
and holding our wind when someone rips a smelly fart
and bopping each other in the head with boxing gloves
and playing pool and rapping and singing and dreaming about the
    future.

we be   talking about   the girls we like.

    I wonder if Bubba and Cubby know that there's something
                            different about me,
        and if they talk about it when I'm not around them.

Bubba is in the corner of the cafeteria with his girlfriend Candy.
he is dark brown round cheek laughing with her about something,
and rocking creased dark blue slacks with black suspenders,
a crisp white button-down shirt, and a silk blue and red striped tie
casket sharp: fresh and clean
he wants to major in business and has been dressing up every day
   this school year,
says he's preparing for his future accounting career.

Cubby, on the other hand, also wants to major in business,
but his wardrobe is far less formal than Bubba's.
his sneakers are *always* the latest of the greatest.
I can always identify him by his fancy footwear.
I spot him walking first class in the lunch line to pay for curly fries,
wearing light blue jeans, an extra-extra-long white T-shirt,
and golden Flightposites that cost a fortune,
but Cubby is a big boy whose family can afford to fly.

whole time, I ain't got enough cash to cover the cost of purchasing
   non-free food.
I gotta wait until next Friday before I get paid from my job at Old
   Navy,
so, I secure my tray of free rectangle pizza
topped with brown chunks of salty, fatty, oily flesh,
an eight-ounce sturdy paper carton full of sweet chocolate milk,
and a sticky butter crunch cookie.

I'm accustomed to eating free lunch.

sometimes, I'll ask Ma for a few bucks before she leaves for work
so that I can buy snacks from the vending machine.
if she's got it, she always gives it,   which ain't too often.
so, I'll usually find a way to scrape up enough nickels and dimes
to rub four quarters together
to buy one of the one-dollar pizza slices our senior class sells after
    school.

        the proceeds go to pay for our prom, which is only two
            months away.

we all sit in a circle surrounded by the rest of the juniors and
    seniors.
it's always extra loud in here.
I pivot my ear perfectly enough to hear Cubby reminding us that a
    representative
from Morgan State University (MSU) will be meeting with
    prospective students
in the guidance office this afternoon.
"oh yeah, I heard about that too, I was gonna go,
but I didn't want to be the only person in there," I lie.
"it wouldn't hurt to hear what he's talking about,
plus, we can skip last period," Cubby says.
we all go, "say less."

suddenly, from somewhere in this cipher of cafeteria chatter
comes the sound of lunch tables screeching across the floor
and every curse from the book of bad words starts ripping through
    the air

like Fourth of July firecrackers.
students are backing themselves against each other,
making a hole in the center,
forming a circle around two boys engaged in fisticuffs.
they are focusing most of their angry energy on punching a target
marked dead center of each other's faces.

these gladiators are from two different neighborhoods
located on two different sides of the same street,
and seem to be having different opinions about way too many
    things,
none of which are things that either of them seem to know
how to settle by simply speaking strong vocabulary.

everyone is yelling, "fight! fight! fight!"
and I'm hoping this brawl don't spread out into a web of sticky
    boundaries
and I am forced to choose where my loyalty lies
based on the location of whatever part of PG land I'm living on,
because my roots are tied much tighter underneath the nearby DC
    soil.

we all breathe in for two Mississippis and then let go of the air
    cumulating within us.
I grab my special notebook and scarf down the cold crusty corner
    of my free lunch pizza
and proceed to the exit doors where our administrators are
    mobilized on the front line,

waiting with their stern faces, and walkie-talkies, and building
    keys, organizing our herd,
while trying to untangle these prizefighters.

CAUGHT UP IN A TRIVIAL TUSSLE OVER TERRITORY.

when we moved to PG in 1990,
I learned quickly that some people who live in *this* "land"
don't always get along with people who represent *that* "village."
and that folks from *that* side of the "glen"
don't get along with individuals who stay in *that* "ridge."
all of this continues to be confusing for me
because the only part of the earth I ever needed to get along with
   is in DC.

I ain't know that I'd have to battle wits with my choice of words
   about
where I am from until some of these PG kids started asking about
   my origin.
they don't know anything about where I was *before* I got here.

they don't know that before my first birthday,
Pop finished airman basic training in Freehold, NJ, and moved all
   of us
to a two-level, four-bedroom house on Bolling Air Force Base in
   southeast DC (the Base).
the Base was a place with a lift gate and security guards who sat

inside of small stations
that asked my cousins, aunts, uncles, and grandparents for photo
    IDs,
just to verify their eligibility for "visitor" passes required for any
    civilian
who wanted to enter the armed sanctuary of familes previously
    stationed
in places like Hawaii, Florida, Texas, and Guam.

they don't know I grew up in a bubble of cookie-cutter homes,
protected from the rest of the nation's capital: a city full of sweet
    chocolate people.
        a government housing project that came with carports and
            playgrounds
        and recreational centers, arcades, and a bowling alley.

they don't know that Ma's side of the family host our reunions in
    Kenilworth Park
        in northeast DC, at the Aquatic Gardens, in Deanwood.
they don't know my great-grandparents spent their lives in Tyler
    House Apartments
and that my great-great-grandparents worked for white folks in
    Georgetown.
they don't know my grandma is a registered dietician at DC
    Village.
they don't know Ma and Pop fell in love at Theodore Roosevelt
    High School.
they don't know me and Tamu transferred from DC public schools.

they don't know our suburban freedom tour has included over a
    dozen addresses.

                                  we are never permanently anywhere.

Ma keeps moving us to different places with complicated names
    that sound like

Arbor Lakes, Country View, Forrest Hill, and Woods Landing

that don't have any real access to view PG's lakes and lands.

truth is, we move around so damn much

that I can't seem to sit still long enough to allow green grass to
    grow underneath my feet.

we've become a dynasty of renters with a legacy of apartment
    leases

spread across a six-mile radius.

I've normalized packing up moving boxes at night with just the
    items I keep in my bedroom,

only to unpack them the following evening in a new unit that was
    somehow better than where we were before.

they don't know that I think Ma is running from her own
    Boogeyperson.

they don't know about the verbal battle between my parents that
    brought us here:

      I was about four years old, earshot of their bedroom on the Base,
              hearing them speaking words to each other that weren't
                            making any sense
              but I was getting the sense that whatever those words
                            meant to them

was a heavy thing that they couldn't seem to lift off their shoulders.
so, they just let the thing linger there long enough to barely
silence their curses
enough to hear me screaming out for their attention.
"I'm right here!" I carved into air molecules,
hoping that atomically, they'd feel something created
from their nucleus
shifting out of their orbit.

or maybe I was thinking too loud inside of my head
because the voice I was pulling on was being suppressed by
some dark force
that I could feel flying around their bedroom walls:
something sticking to the white paint.
something peeling back the heaviness blinking beneath Ma's eyes.
something more than her makeup could make up.
and It kept looking at me from behind the first soul
that I'd ever seen.
some black, faceless monster performing cartwheels
up and down her cheeks
and I was scared of monsters   so scared.
loud things. ringing. burning. shouting.

I remember hearing Ma singing, "it's okay, baby," but all I could
taste was salt.
perhaps I was peeling away too.
I ain't have enough volume to compete with the performance of
bad feelings

projecting out of my parents' mouths.
all that fussing   at each other,
as if, they ain't create me and Tamu and our entire world   together.

them: us: we all start swirling into a category five storm
of sharp words.
sounding like thunder and lightning ripping the roof off our home,
shattering glass windows with sticks and stones
stuffed with dynamite that were designed to explode, crush egos,
and break apart bones buried deep in the basement.

I assumed all that bass buried deep in Pop's voice meant
something was out of tune with the melancholic melody foaming
at Ma's mouth,
because without wings, he sprouted feathers and flew far away
from their bedroom   forever
and landed on a pillow where he talks to some other woman.

I NEED TO SIT STILL IN PEACE.

I gotta find some place where my quiet freedom can exist
     uninterrupted.
and I wonder if those feuding Black boys are finding solace in
     solitude,
as they're forced by administrators to sit silently in the detention
     room,
chewing on words they still need to say to each other about what
     happened
after being questioned and reprimanded for fighting their battles.

they damn sure ain't in here with the rest of us Talented and
     Gifted (TAG) students
crammed inside a tiny dimly lit conference room outside of Ms.
     Zbornak's office.
          all of us chosen to be present for this meeting
          solely because we're a part of some school agenda
          that shines a bright light on our unexplainably dim academic
               aptitudes and abilities.
                         I guess the rest of DuVal High's students
                    are intentionally being left out and far behind
          to fend for themselves in the wild world of life after graduation.

Ms. Zbornak is an oak-tree-tall, paper-thin, white woman
with lips like the subtraction sign,
whom I've never seen stand up from her desk.
and I don't think she cares that her ash-white roots
don't match the maple ends of her stringy straight hair.

truth is, I've never sought her counsel about the things
that the Boogeyman stuffs inside my backpack pockets,
and makes me carry around in school all day.
I've never hinted to her about the things that It makes me fight for
    in my dreams either.
nor do I inform her about the playground bully boys
and my parents' divorce, and Pop's addiction, and Ma's penniless
    pocketbook.

and I sure ain't asked for Ms. Zbornak's guidance about
what my life could be like once I am unattached from Ma's
    outsides,
so I'm grateful when she introduces us to Mr. Fiasco from MSU's
    Office of Admissions.

he says MSU is a small historically Black university (HBCU) in
    Baltimore, MD,
and that it's a place where only the best, brightest, and most
    brilliant Black minds belong.
he says their primary mission is the education of Black Americans
and that upon acceptance, we can expect to be challenged and
    supported beyond
what our dreams make us believe is possible

for ourselves, our families, and our communities.

      whole time, my family been pouring these *exact* words into me
          since I came out in the world as a shooting star on fire.

he gives us a college-ready checklist,
while I, without blue ink pen or yellow notepad,
    but a rock-solid gold memory,
internally respond to each of his outward calls:

"now, all of you have at least a 3.5 GPA,
so, you're already in good position,
just have Ms. Zbornak send us your transcripts."
                      okay, that's easy.
"you'll need to make sure you have a letter of recommendation
written by at least two of your teachers."
            okay, Mr. Marshall, but shit who else?
                definitely not Ms. Nyland.
"you'll need *at least* a 1000 combined SAT score
and a minimum of 550 on the English portion."
          shit, I gotta study *extra* hard tonight.
            I don't get much sleep anyway,
      might as well make use of the time I spend awake.

I look at Tolu and she is looking at Mr. Fiasco,
so I look back at him too.

"oh, and the application fee is fifty dollars."
           shit. I'm broke and so is Ma.

"but I will waive this fee,
if you promise me today, by signing this information sheet,
that you will mail in all of your documents by the end of the
    month."
                                    ah! where is the pen, my brotha?!
then, Mr. Fiasco tells us to make sure we complete the
Free Application for Federal Student Aid (FAFSA),
which could award us grants and lend us money toward cutting
    college costs.

                                    how much is the tuition?
                                what if I get in, but can't pay?
                                    I should ask, but . . .
                                        my stomach hurts.
Mr. Fiasco says he knows some of us (me) are applying past their
    final deadline,
so, we should consider ourselves blessed for this opportunity.
        Pop always says that things happen for a reason and a season.

then, Mr. Fiasco gives us all gift bags that include an ink pen, a
    notepad, a coffee mug,
and a blue-and-orange-colored T-shirt with a screen-printed
    picture of their mascot: a bear.
                            DuVal tigers and MSU bears, oh my,
            I wonder if there are some lions in my academic future.

Mr. Fiasco closes by saying, "I heard a rumor that a few of you
are coming down with a seriously dangerous and contagious case
    of senioritis

that's causing you to not feel like doing anything else this year
that will positively contribute toward your life after graduation.
but be aware, my teenage cubs, we are not interested in accepting
    lazy bears
who prefer hibernation over graduation."
we are chirping like crickets, but Mr. Fiasco manages to squeeze
    some juicy laughter
out of his dry-ass joke,
which must've come from some place in his lungs
where he stores the limited humor that's meant solely for awkward
    moments
whenever adults speak *at* youth.

then again, senioritis is a cool concept for my talent show poem.
                I write the idea down in the margin of my paper
and tell Mr. Fiasco that he can expect to receive my application in
                                        the mail.

I CAN DO THIS.

"so, what did y'all think about what Mr. Fiasco said?" Cubby asks
    Bubba and me
as we walk across the street and down the road to where each of us
    live, differently.
"yo, he sold me," I say, "I'm absolutely gonna apply
now that I know there is some last-minute chance I could get in.
although I'm still not sure what I want to major in."

                    I think back to Pop quoting 1 Corinthians 2:9:
                                about eyes not seeing.
                                about ears not hearing.
                                about the hearts of men.
                            about all that God has for me.
Bubba asks, with a slight snicker,
"Tone Capone, what are you gonna do with your poetry,
write some commercial jingles for a living?"
                this is the nickname he gave me.
his joke about the possibilities for my poems to be of use for both
    college and a career
is causing all of us to laugh really hard at me.
"I'm kidding, bro," Bubba affirms.

"I feel the same way you do, Tōne-loc," Cubby says.

        this is the nickname he gave me.

        their words, twisting my name around like this feels

           like love.

Bubba says, "shit, if anything, we are all Black kings out here,

so our greatness is kinda inevitable."

                        he is so wise.

Cubby continues, "I already know I'm destined to be an

    entrepreneur,

think about it, why is it that we can't get *both* delicious pizza

aaaannnnddddd perfectly made buffalo chicken from the same

    place?"

    despite his mother's delicious home cooking, Cubby is a

        carryout aficionado.

    he knows which places got the extra crispy french fries

        and crunchy juicy wings with mambo sauce,

        and steak and cheese eggrolls with real beef and melty

           cheese.

"it's a supply-and-demand issue, I'm telling you," he says,

"my future food business is gonna solve that problem, just wait and

    see."

I chime in, "you can hire me to write the poem for your commercial

    jingle."

we all laugh really hard, then, Bubba gets serious,

"the question we're gonna have to answer is,

what are we going to do about *our* ladies when the time comes to choose schools?"

Cubby doesn't have a girlfriend, so he ain't saying nothing.

I respond, without looking in either of their direction,

"yeah, Blu and I are just gonna leave it in God's hands."

                      as if there is a human form of something so divine.

"I'll see her at choir rehearsal tonight and I'm sure we'll be talking
    about it *again*.

besides, I think she's applying to MSU too."

"word? that'd be dope," Bubba says without further inquisition.

he continues, "I've got my eyes on Temple University in Philly,

but I think Candy wants to go to MSU, she was really inspired by
    Mr. Fiasco's spiel too."

Cubby says, "I guess we'll all just have to wait and see,

who knows, we might end up at MSU together, Tōne-loc,

and then we can travel up to see Bubba in Philly."

"all of this sounds like a wonderful dream, fellas," I say underneath
    my breath,

"again, I'm just gonna leave it in God's hands."

WE SPLIT INTO SEPARATE
BUT EQUAL PIECES AT THIS POINT

my best boy-friends live in townhomes located inside of a quiet
   community
that is just a few minutes' walk from our apartment complex.
to get to their houses, I walk out the back door of our apartment
   building
and slide through a human-sized hole that is diagonally cut into
an eight-foot-high barbed wire fence.
once I'm through, skin slightly scratched white and scraped up,
I follow a flat-footed dirt trail that wraps around a wooded path
where I've seen bats fly after tiny bugs at night.

      I guess some of my neighbors have a history of making this
         same pilgrimage too.

I say, "peace, brothas," while lifting my right arm up toward my chin,
and twisting my palm toward my face,
while pinning both my pinky and ring fingers down with the tip
   of my thumb,
and then, show my signature smile.

I walk home imagining the college experience being like
   A Different World:

I see myself becoming a goofy romantic scholar with righteous
    speech like Dwayne Wayne,
wearing my colorfully twisted Cross Colours caps
with the price tags still in place and tossed to the side
and my sunshades flipped out and opened up toward the sky.

it'd be pretty dope if Blu and I both get into the same school.
although she would be nothing at all like Whitley Gilbert.
ain't nothing pink, dainty, sassy, or super soft about her.
but ain't nothing gray concrete, cement, or stone about her either.

Blu is all bright red, plum purple, dandelion orange, sky blue, and
    sunflower yellow.
an artistic free spirit who paints pictures of beautiful Black babies
    all day,
and willingly watches NBA games after school,
with full knowledge of the players, stats, and court rules.
        she is the only person I can play basketball with and have fun.

Blu reads poetry written by Black and brown women:
Nikki Giovanni, June Jordan, Audre Lorde, Maya Angelou,
Gwendolyn Brooks, and Lucille Clifton.
she raps and sings the soulful-sounding poetic lyricism
flowing inside of rap, R&B, and neo-soul music made by them
    too:
Mary J. Blige, Lauryn Hill, Erykah Badu, Jill Scott,
India Arie, Angie Stone, Brandy, SWV, and Zhané.

in my different world, I imagine Blu being spirally Freddie Brooks
because she would be all wise mouth and clear sharp mind.
she would also be an artistic Lena James,
all fashion forward and absolutely unafraid of confrontation.

the thing is, Blu got a leg up on the college stuff.
her parents are upper-middle-class Black folks
with BMWs, college degrees, stocks, bonds, and foreign
    currencies.

WHOLE TIME, COLLEGE FEELS SO FOREIGN TO ME.

I walk in our apartment and there is no sign of life,
I call Ma on her desk phone at the Pentagon
where she works as an executive assistant for some federal
    government agency.

I usually let her know when I get home ever since my sister and I
    were latchkey kids.
without Pop's fatherly financial contribution to our single-parent
    household,
Ma chose the survival of *their* children: us: we,
over his selfish-ass addictions to poisoned cocaine and pillow
    talking to other women.
so, she stretches beyond her Black motherhood means by working
    part-time shifts
in the dark evenings at dozens of different discount department
    stores,
running cash registers stocking shelves and serving customers.

"hey baby, how was school?" Ma asks, sounding like a playful
    hummingbird's song.
I respond, "honestly, it was pretty cool.

I met this guy who works at MSU who said he'd waive my college
    application fee
as long as I submit everything by the deadline."

"how much is the tuition?" Ma asks,
already calculating the total number of penny holes holding up her
    pocketbook.
"are they offering you any money?
you know I don't really have anything to spare right now,
especially because your father is still behind on child-support
    payments."

"yeah, Ma, I already know," I offer as medicine for her still-healing
    wounds.
"there's something called a FAFSA that we gotta complete
    together
and it is supposed to help reduce some of my college costs.
don't worry about it, Ma, I'll figure something out when the time
    comes."

"I know you will, baby," she affirms.
"one thing I know about my son is, he's gonna find a way to
    accomplish his goals."

    I am showing all my teeth to the phone,
        hoping she can hear how much I believe her when she
            reminds me to trust in myself.
    Ma has always been my biggest fan:

the head captain of my cheerleading team,
always rooting for me to win whatever it is that I'm battling
against.

I remind her that I have choir rehearsal tonight and will be home
later.
although I already know I'll be awake when she comes home after
second shift,
I'm used to being awake most nights, staring at the Boogeyman
breathing hard and heavy inside of my bedroom closet.

I am "man of the house."
this has been my title since we moved from the Base to PG
without Pop,
and Ma says that in addition to taking out the trash,
wiping down the toilet seat, cleaning and grooming my growing
body,
I am also tasked with defending our home
protecting her and Tamu from predators.
so, I usually get up in the middle of the night
just to double-check that Ma put the bolt lock on the door
and took her eyeglasses off before falling asleep to the sound of her
TV's white noise.

I end my call with Ma and fix a grilled cheese and pot of chicken-
flavored ramen,
walk to my bedroom and flop facedown on my bed
and reach my hands underneath the box spring.

amongst the clutter of lost rubber bands, half-bitten pencil erasers,
    soda can tops,
underarm deodorant caps, and unpaired white tube socks,
I dig out my sky blue off-brand sneaker box.
I turn myself over and look up to make sure that I shut and locked
    my door.
although I am home alone, I prefer to keep this part of myself
    private.
I lift open the lid to reveal my hoard.

I EXHALE FOR THE FIRST TIME TODAY

my poems: all the written-down dictations of words I think about,
but am too scared to say out loud.
all my truths   right here, spread out in ink, turned inside out,
and splattered on sheets of notebook paper that I tore off from the
    metal coil core
that once held their spine in alignment.

I keep my poems here because honestly,
I don't have a real reason to throw them away.
everything that makes them whole came directly from several
    different parts of me,
and so, I go to them as a strategy for figuring out answers to
    questions
that I ask myself about myself and the world around me,
when no one is around to hear me thinking inside of my own
    head.
especially when I cannot pinpoint the root cause
of some strong feeling that's weighing me down.
I'll pen my emotions in poems by painting pictures with words
that describe what the feeling looks and sounds like.
then, I'll read what I wrote to myself over and over,

until I can imagine the story that's being told inside of the stanzas.

somehow, that process helps me create a moving picture of my
    poems,
and I'll watch myself searching inside of them for language
that makes whatever that feeling is   less heavy.
    spending time with my poems must be like those therapy
        sessions
    that I see white folks go to in the movies,
    except I am the only person counseling my emotions,
    sans couch and an expensive hourly rate.

I pull out the poem I wrote today (sometime after midnight)
and read it out loud in rotation,
wondering what it is that I am trying to say,
and to whom am I trying to say all of this to?
because it's definitely about me and absolutely not exactly about
    Blu.

UNTITLED

How upset you must've been
all night, as you tossed and turned
I can understand how hot you felt
as the nightmare in you burned.
You are so innocent,
but not good enough to sleep.
What was on your conscience
that made your unconscious weep?
I can understand how painful
your body must be,
for you lay awake the entire adventure,
at least until the stroke of three.
The weight that lives under your eyes
is heavier than guilt
oh sweetheart,
I can imagine how you feel.
Because the connection of our soul
will make the Sand Man a believer
for with all the truth in my heart
and the dreams I had
I, myself, did not sleep either.

How upset you must've been
all night as you tossed and turned
I can understand how hot you felt
as the nightmare in you burned
You are so innocent, but not good
enough to sleep
What was on your conciounse that
made your unconsuas weep
I can understand how painful your
body must be
For you lied awake the entire
adventure at least the stroke of three
The weight that lives under your
eyes is heavier than guilt
Oh sweetheart I can imagine how you
~~felt~~ feeled
Because the connection of our soul
will make the sandman a believer
For with all the truth in my heart
and the dreams I had, I myself did not
sleep either

STILL UNSURE WHAT I AM FIGURING OUT

I place the poem back in the box when I hear a car horn beeping.
I look through my bedroom window blinds facing the parking lot
and see it's one of my best girl-friends, Ebby, and her mother,
    Auntye P.
they're my usual ride to youth choir rehearsal and church.
    Ma and Tamu don't attend,
        although, I've never asked them to join us.

I hop, skip, and jump my way down our apartment building's
    stairwell
and slide in the back seat of an iridescent lavender and baby blue
    four-door sedan.
Auntye P is rocking her usual short salt-n-pepa fade,
and a denim shirt, starched extra crispy, with the collar popped.
she is blasting "Diamonds and Pearls" by Prince and the New
    Power Generation
on her car's crackling stereo system
while pumping both of her hands high up in the air,
and every bit of her shoulders bouncing around: her signature
    dance.

Auntye P is a loving spirit with gigantic vibrant energy
and a sweet buoyancy floating in her voice that always seems to
    soothe the weary
whenever I feel like no one else can help me understand my *why*.
        for real for real, I think she be knowing more about me
        than I know about myself sometimes.

"hey Tony, what's going on, boy-friend?" she says, in her typical
    cheerful voice.
to Auntye P, I am some hybrid child, who is both her nephew and
    Ebby's only sibling.
"hi brother," Ebby adds, reaching her body from the front passenger
    seat toward the back,
hugging me around my neck.
"what's up, y'all?" I respond.
Auntye P says, "you are looking rough, do we need to make a trip
    to H Street
and get a fried fish sandwich from Horace and Dickies?"
        she is holding her entire mouth open, exposing the slight gap
            between her top front teeth,
        smiling all the joy I need in my life.
that does sound delicious, but my face doesn't budge,
instead I look at myself reflected in the rearview mirror and
    indeed,
my battery looks damn near drained.

"Mom, stop it!" Ebby interjects into her mother's sweet
    interrogation.

"I'm doing okay, I guess," I lie. they know.

I turn the faucet on without any waterworks.
"it's just that figuring out the college thing is intensifying by the
    hour,
and all I need is a couple of minutes to catch my breath,
so that I can think clearly for a few seconds.

"plus, I gotta retake the SAT in the morning, because after two of
    my best tries,
I didn't get a 1200 like Ms. Nyland said I needed.
Mr. Fiasco, from MSU, said that he can make some magic happen
if I score at least 1000 points, but more than half of those should
    be in English
and my standard ain't too good.

"and, I don't know how the hell I'm gonna pay for all of this shit."
                Auntye P don't mind when Ebby and I use curse words
                        when simple vocabulary ain't exclamatory enough
                                to mean what we're really trying to say.

"and I don't even know if I want to go to MSU in the first place
        I don't even know where it is.
            what does the campus look like?
            what am I going to major in?
plus, I gotta write this poem for the senior talent show."
                                    I can't inhale.
                                    my stomach hurts.
"breathe, Tony!" Ebby fills into my well.

"first of all, you're one of the smartest people I know,
so, there's no question whether you'll go or not.
second of all . . ."
"but, Ebby . . ."
"hush up, Tony!" she shouts,
while continuing to pour more love inside all the places
that I believe are far too deep for saturation.

"second of all, you're the best poet in the world
and I ain't saying that just because you're my brother, it's the truth.
I still have the poem you wrote for me in eighth grade
the day after me and my mother left *that man who will not be
    named.*
    you told me that it was okay to wear my emotions all over my
        sleeves
    and that I could borrow one of yours
        to wipe the boogers off right after I sneezed.
it's not easy to laugh while in pain and mean it.
you're just a good-natured person, brother,
you've just gotta believe that good things are going to happen for
    you."

                                    she punctured right through me.
"Ebby, but I don't . . ."
"didn't I say hush?
third of all, I've already accepted admission to Towson University
    (TU),
which ain't nothing but a fifteen-minute drive to MSU,
and we just got my car tuned up for college,

so, *when* you get into MSU, we will be seeing each other all the
    time."
"do you really think so?" I ask.
my aunt-mother and sister girl-friend both go, "uh duh!"

Ebby continues, "plus ain't that many Black folks at TU,
which means I'll be needing to see another familiar face
more than every once in a while to sustain my sanity."

Auntye P echoes her only child's affirmations,
"Tony, you always know that if you ever need anything, Ebby and
    I are here for you."

I am filling up.

MY HEAD IS BRIGHT AND CLEAR

we pull up to Good Luck Church (GLC), where Blu is waiting at
the main entrance.
Auntye P tells me and Ebby that she'll be back to pick us up at
7:30 p.m.,
which is exactly twelve and a half hours before I need to be at
DuVal High to take the SAT.
I already know that I ain't gonna get any sleep.

"hey Tony!" Blu says with a big bright smile.
I bounce back at her brilliant shine by reaching my arms around
her shoulders
until my hands connect across her back
and then, I squeeze us toward one another for three solid seconds.
"hey, Blu!" I respond.
"you always give the best hugs," she says, followed by a blushing
giggle.

"what's up, girl?" Ebby asks.
"chilling, waiting on you two to get here,
y'all know we're always the last ones at rehearsal
and I ain't wanna walk in by myself."

we all laugh at Blu's honesty.
"true dat," Ebby and I both say in unison.

the three of us quietly shuffle our way inside the sanctuary where
the rest of the youth choir members are already standing up in the
    pulpit,
in the ascending pews, organized by their respective sound
    sections.
the choir is mimicking musical notes that Kirk, our choir director,
is playing from behind the keyboard.
he looks over at the three of us,
and without adjusting his fingers from the keys,
shifts the direction of his eyeballs from left to right,
as a nonverbal signal that we should proceed to our sections and
    follow suit.

I sing tenor, and join the other fellas
and Kierra, the only girl amongst us who can sing just low enough
to not get lost in the top or bottom of Kirk's musical notes.
we are positioned in the middle, toward the front of the baritones,
but to the left of the sopranos, and to the right of the altos.

I've been singing for GLC's youth choir since the end of sophomore
    year
after Ebby and Blu invited me to join them for rehearsal one
    evening after school.
they've been members here for years.
they told me to hang out in the back and listen.

which is what I did
until I lost myself somewhere amongst the sounds of their voices
I did not know that harmonies *like that* existed.
I was surprised that melodies like *that* could billow from their
    mouths.
all of their eyes were shut extra tight,
none of them could see themselves singing with each other like
    that.

I didn't know it was okay to sing loud in a church,
or that it was cool to let your hands float in the air for freedom
    like *that*.
didn't know that Black boys and our varying levels of vibrato and
    bass
could find a religious place to belt out our joyful noise like *that*.

didn't know we could become comfortable displaying out loud
all the emotions that I be writing about in silence like *that*.

they had no filter and I did not apply for an audition,
I just moved myself and my entire spirit up a few more rows,
and started taking cues from Kirk, who was actively listening to
    my voice,
discovering wherever it was within this atmosphere he heard my
    pitch belonging best.
he pointed: tenor.

meanwhile his wife, Yolanda, was down in front facing all of us,

rocking her entire body, mouthing the words to each song
ahead of the time that we are supposed to sing them.
I was memorizing lyrics and melodies only a few seconds before
she allowed me to let them fly off my tongue,
in sync and on the same runway with everyone else,
who, Kirk says, should've been doing the exact same thing.
Yolanda's hands gave me spoken word instruction,
teaching my voice what it is supposed to do:
higher   softer   whisper
        louder   lower
                rise   fall
                        SING WITH EVERYTHING YOU'VE GOT!
sing nothing at all.

I found my own sound amongst the masses
and I was no longer able to locate the parts of myself that scared
        the shit out of me.
it was as if I could see the words forming themselves inside my
        belly,
climbing out of my throat and escaping out of me   free.

                        Ms. Nyland could benefit teaching like this in class.
                perhaps then I could demonstrate my fluency of the American
                                                standard,
                        if given the opportunity to both write *and* perform my words.

SINGING BE LIKE PRAYING.

we've been rehearsing songs for Sunday's service
and I'm feeling like there is a bubble of joy ready to pop open
    inside me somewhere.
Kirk tells us to close our eyes as we sing the lyrics to the sermonic
    selection:

> Lord, I hear of showers of blessing.
> thou art scattering full and free.
> showers the thirsty souls refreshing

closing my eyes tight like this,
when singing these gospel songs with all my heart,
I know that eventually, Kirk is gonna speed up the tempo,
and then the drummer is gonna pump that bass harder,
and then Yolanda is gonna make the whole choir clap, stomp, and
    sway a lot deeper.
and then, one of us is gonna start hollering for joy a lot louder.

next thing you know, we'll all be creating a circumference of
    celestial noise
before Kirk signals for the musicians to stop playing their
    instruments,

so that he can just hear us: the choir,
calling out to God with greater purpose.
all of us, praying for something in psalm
that we all need divine intervention for,

"and God, I need to get into college.
look, I don't know if you're listening to what I'm thinking,
while I'm singing directly to you right now,
but I'm gonna need for you to rain down the right answers on this
    SAT.

"I need you to flood Ma's wallet with currency
that's worth more than her overwhelming wave of bills,
    so that she can finally get the rest she deserves.
and so that I can afford to become a goofy romantic college
    scholar,
who writes beautiful poetry on the page
and performs them with power on the stage."

"with Blu?" God asks, in a voice that sounds just like mine.
"I don't know," I respond.
    "but I do know that *you* know
that the Boogeyman ain't never left my side.
and I don't know why you continue to allow It to stick around,
but if for the umpteenth time   I did something to upset you,
I'm so very sorry.

"and if it's because of that *other* thing,

which I'm scared to speak about inside of my head,
                especially while singing inside of your house,
then that's something that I really don't know
what to do about.
you already know that I came out of Ma *the way that I am.*"

God asks, "what's the truth?"
I respond, "I'm terrified that the Boogeyman is gonna hear
what I've been thinking about certain boys
and what happens to my heartbeat when I'm around some of them.
and God, you know that's been the case ever since I met Darin."

I WAS THIRTEEN WHEN ALL THIS STARTED.

Darin was the sixteen-year-old nephew of a woman in Ma's village,
who came to our apartment one summer afternoon.
Tamu and I were playing a few games of blind man's bluff with
    him
and Dallas, one of my friends from middle school who lived in our
    complex.

Blind man's bluff is like hide-and-seek,
but the person who is "it" must wear a blindfold and try to tag all
    of us in the darkness.
Tamu is "it."
Darin, Dallas, and I go hide in my bedroom closet
                                    where the Boogeyman lives.

I'm squatting down to avoid detection,
which also makes me eye level with Darin's waist.
he is standing up straight and tall.
I look up and see that he has black curly hairs
covering his upper lip and around his chin.
he is peeking through the cracks of the wooden closet blinds to see
    if Tamu is coming.

I feel my body turn up to at least 350 degrees Fahrenheit.
"must be a fever," I thought, because I had become flammable
and started burning myself up from within.
I try to keep calm and quiet,
while using my right palm to fan a light wind over my face,
hoping to circulate some oxygen into my life
before I dry up like a bundle of sticks wrapped together that could
    combust
and ignite into flames at any second.
I felt like I was always one breath away from sparking that
    cramped space
into a furnace that set itself on fire.

Darin doesn't see me watching the sweat beads sliding down his
    mahogany forehead
and landing heavy inside the cotton fibers of his ribbed white tank
    top,
which is a tad bit torn around the nape and across his left nipple.

suddenly, Tamu flings the door open with her blindfold still
    twisted on tight
reaching her arms out to tag Dallas,
who was hunched down on the other side of Darin.

suddenly, a funky odor releases in the air and flies first class one
    way inside my nose
I inhale myself inside out.
ZAP! everything about me becomes electric.

Tamu screams out, "I got you!" while grabbing on to Darin's left
    leg.

I see the Boogeyman peeking out from a crack in the corner near
    Darin's knee
and I scream, "oh shit!"
I pop up on my feet and dart past Tamu.
whatever that scent was turned the circuit on to power up my
    sexual system
and then I pray to you, God, that Darin doesn't try to tag me in
    the next round.

I've been fascinated by that smell for as long as forever has been
    forever.

"so, you see, you're the only one who knows about all of this.
and it was just last Sunday, when Pastor Jenkins was preaching
    about gay people,
through *his* biblical interpretation of:
Genesis 19 / Judges 19 / Leviticus 18:22, 20:13 / 1 Corinthians 6:9 /
    1 Timothy 1:10
and I don't want to burn in hell forever,
especially for something I don't even know that I am."

AMEN

"what's going on with you, Tony?" Blu asks, after finishing our
    choir's close-out prayer.
"I look over from the alto section and see you in the tenor area
pouring your whole heart out all over the pew.
is there something going on that you want to talk to me about?
you know that I'll listen."

I know she will.

"ah Blu, you know me *too* well sometimes.
there's just a lot on my mind about college
and a few other things that I don't even want to get into right now.
I just need to get back home and study for the SAT in the
    morning,
but I promise, I'm good."

I'm not. she knows.

"by the way, didn't you say something about applying to MSU?" I
    ask.
"yeah, well, you know both my mom and stepdad went to HBCUs
so, there's a bit of an obligation on my end to at least apply there.
plus, they've got a dope fine arts program
and I've been working on my senior-class portfolio

to include some of my paintings in the applications."
                              damn, I must be the only person
                    in the entire universe who is unprepared for college.
"that'd be perfect for you, Blu!"
                              I want her to give me a hug so badly.
         although everyone in youth choir knows that we "go together,"
      we don't be all public about ourselves, and especially not at church.

"have you decided on a major yet?" she asks.
"I know you've been struggling with that."

         I think about Bubba, and how certain he is about his life.
              so much so that he's unapologetically wearing himself
                                         on the outside.
                    and then I think about Cubby, solving some
                         supply-and-demand problem
                    with perfect pizza and spicy buffalo wings.

         I picture myself as an adult dressed in a navy blue suit
              with a white-collar button-down shirt, a red tie,
            and shiny black shoes that have two dangling tassels,
       and I'm standing next to a flip chart pad, holding a pointer stick,
              giving a presentation about something important
              inside of a conference room in New York City.

              I look like I'm engaged in what I'm doing
       and that I am trying to love this imaginary career created from my
                              college education,

but the conference room windows reflect direct sunlight
onto the side of my face where I am not smiling.
I am staring at the Boogeyman disguised in business blues.

I got the blues, but don't tell Blu.
instead, I say, "I'm still tryna figure that part out."
she looks at me and says, "it's okay, Tony, I believe you."

I HOPE GOD HEARD ME

Ma ain't home yet from second shift and ain't no food cooked.
I microwave a pepperoni Hot Pocket and head to my bedroom
where I plan to collect my thoughts before burying myself
deep in the quick sinking sands of studying for this stupid SAT.

I gotta walk by Tamu's room to get to my den-sized sleeping
    quarters,
she has the door closed and I can hear her talking to someone on
    the phone.
I knock: one tap, then three taps followed by two more,
which is our way of signaling to each other that a truce has been
    drawn
between our occasional sibling rivalry.
    I come in peace.

"hey Punkin," she says, while opening me up to her room,
showing the full depth of dimples burrowed into both sides of her
    almond face.
her smile is pure white, straight, shiny, and sincere, just like Ma's.
and for the last five years, she has been wearing her hair short
    enough
for the entire world to see every single and solitary black strand

growing out of her coconut-shell scalp.

"hey Tamu, don't mean to disturb you,
just wanna know if you need the computer tonight?
I gotta study for my SAT tomorrow and write my personal
    statement."
"nope, I don't need it tonight," she responds,
"but wait a second, I've got something for you."
she reaches behind her door and pulls out a large white book with
    a picture of white kids standing in front of a gray building
    complete with four concrete columns,
a cobblestone entrance, a clock tower, and a hanging brass bell.
she says someone gave it to her last year and that it's got a bunch of
    stuff about
university rankings, college majors, student clubs, tuition and fees.
                    whole time, MSU is the only option on the table,
                        but I know she means well.

I almost fall over catching the enormous source of answers in my
    left hand
while trying to hold on to my not-so-hot Hot Pocket with my
    right.
she goes, "I figured my little brother's brilliant brain could make
    use of this
because I know college means a lot to you."

                    I've never asked Tamu if she had dreams
                    of being our family's first college student.
                            we've always been close.

us: siblings barely one year apart, raised like twins,
always figuring ourselves out apart from each other.
still do sometimes.
although, I'm learning that my power resides somewhere between
the things that rumble in my gut,
and the things beckoning to fly out of my mouth.

I think Tamu is still figuring out the source of her
supernatural strength.
I wonder if she knows that thunder is caused by the
rapid expansion
of the air surrounding the path of a lightning bolt
and that a lightning bolt is an electric discharge
between the atmosphere and the ground.
so perhaps, she sparks all the energy,
because I know I bring all the noise.

I wonder what we'll be like when we're apart
that's if, of course, I get in.

Tamu has always been Ma's co-captain of my cheerleading team.
I am filling up and respond, "aw, thanks, Tamu!"
we do a little fist bump explosion, and she says, "alright, well good
luck studying tonight
and don't forget to eat something in the morning before your test."

she don't know my stomach be hurting.

I'M BARELY COLLEGE PREPARED.

I walk into our dining room and sit down inside one of the
milk chocolate rotating dining chairs on wheels
that comes from the same set of four we had on the Base.
then I pull myself up to the computer
sitting in the corner of our apartment window.

I stack my SAT practice book on top of the one that Tamu
    gave me,
and place them both on our dining room table
next to my glass of tropical fruit punch Kool-Aid.
my notebook full of Mr. Marshall's words   and all their
    weight
is sitting firmly and within reach.
I officially look the part of an actor playing the role
of a high school student who is serious about going to college,
but I don't know how to perform without a screenplay to read
    from.

I turn the power button on to our family's PC
and wait for the black screen on the white monitor to stop
    scrolling binary digits,

before it displays a desktop with wallpaper that looks like a giant
    desert
holding dry space for icons on the right side.

I pull out the SAT book and retrieve the CD-ROM taped to the
    back cover
and slide it into the slot.
I am greeted with a bright screen asking me to choose "Math" or
    "Critical Reasoning."
I select the area that I believe I am actually the highest, but always
    seem to score the lowest.

the first task I am to complete
is reading a paragraph about something I truly do not care about,
and then respond to a particular prompt,
by selecting the right answer from a set of multiple choices.
some of these examples inform me there may be more than one
    correct answer,
which means I must decide to select one, or two, or a few,
or all of them together, or none of them at all.
I try to eliminate the ones that are obviously wrong, so that I have
    less to worry about,
but I keep forgetting what I previously read.

I can't do this.
my stomach hurts.
I decide to look for some guidance inside the SAT practice book.
I open the first chapter and read *verbatim* the words that are
    beaming from the screen.

and there's a section called "hints" with clues for figuring all this
    nonsense out.
damn, Ms. Nyland is right, all the answers *are* here!
but I can't memorize this shit by tomorrow.
for real for real, I'm not sure this approach is gonna help me learn
    anything useful at all.

I wish I knew how to discover answers by using my own way of
                                                            knowing,
                perhaps then all of it would make common sense.

                    I feel like I be thinking in curves and circles
            that don't align with the rigid squares and bone-straight lines
                        that schools be requiring me to draw from.

frustrated, I power off the PC and look at my frowned-up
and defeated face reflecting from the black screen.
I'm terrified of not getting into college because I don't have
    another plan for my life.
I'm too afraid to admit that I am not willing to accept
that the only possibilities for my freedom to exist
means that a college life   can't be it,
or that being too Black   can't be it,
or that being gay   can't be it.

I move my eyes away from the monitor and walk toward my room
so I can go deal with the Boogeyman and all Its bullshit.

MY ANXIETY IS BURNING.

I gently close my bedroom door and pull out the full-body-length
   mirror
I've been lugging around to almost every place we've lived.
    I store it in there after getting dressed,
     instead of keeping it laid against the wall facing the right side
      of my bed,
     because whenever I start thinking badly about myself like
      this,
     I become the Boogeyman,
     and I'm a lot scarier to look at in the darkness.

in addition to praying to God and singing out to Jesus and dancing
   with the Holy Ghost,
and walking my path toward salvation at GLC,
I have another method for face-to-face fighting my fears.
and it involves sourcing the spiritual power that I am finding in
   my poems
to help me combat all that unnecessary negative self-talk.

taking out the mirror is the first part of my ritual for finding a
   way to fall asleep
soundly enough to dream peacefully about my purpose.

I learned how to do this during sophomore year,
after Blu, Tiffy, Ebby, Auntye P, and I went on a weekend cabin
    trip to Sugarloaf Mountain:

it was not the first time I went to places with my girl-friends as the
    only boy in our group.
all our parents trusted we were operating as a responsible and
    platonic lifelong unit.

after learning to ski the bunny slope without tumbling in the snow
and avoiding hitting the base with my face,
we sat in a circle around a real wood-burning fireplace.
it was five minutes to midnight and Auntye P left hours ago
to do something that she didn't tell us about,
but she gave us plenty of cash to order pizza,
and perhaps by mistake, also left a four-pack of blackberry wine
    coolers.

"see, I told y'all that it'd be sweet!" Tiffy said,
as we all lowered the cold plum-colored alcohol from our lips.
        as if pouring a libation down our throats.
"okay, y'all know I'm into witches and wizards and warlocks and
    fortune-telling
and tarot cards and Disney princesses, Egyptian queens, and
    Greek goddesses, right?"
we all nod our heads at her truth, followed by a series of chuckling
    sneers.
she continues, "well, I read about a spell for removing bad energy
    from your life

in *Gloss Magazine* the other day that I think we should try,
and it involves writing our fears away."

she turned on Tupac's "Keep Ya Head Up"
and told us to write how we felt about the scary stuff haunting our
    dreams
and to do so in whatever form made the most sense.
it only took two seconds before I lost track of the thoughts escaping
    my brain
        the ones about my lack of college choices
        the ones about the girls and boys and God and my parents'
            voices.
        I tried hard to usher them toward freedom found on the
            page.

when the song ended, Tiffy said we didn't have to share what we
    wrote
                                        and so none of us did.
but she had us write a name to describe our fear on a tiny piece of
    notebook paper.
I wrote: "the Boogeyman."
then, we folded our phobias in half,
    and then in half again
        and then we rolled them over once more
before tossing our troubles into the roaring furnace
and watching our burdens burn to ashes.
        stripping our Its of their superficial powers to scare us.

I KNOW EXACTLY WHAT TO DO

while staring at the real-life picture of myself in my bedroom
    mirror,
I reach inside my book bag, grab hold of my journal,
and turn to the twenty-second page,
then I start to think,
and with my black ink
I begin to sink myself into the paper,
pressing down each word
as if each letter is an incantation for invoking an inner source of
    light
with rays as hot as the sun's surface,
and that burst out of my body.

I whisper, "I don't know why you don't believe
that you're as bright as one billion diamonds sparkling in daylight
in the middle of Times Square,
but if you're trying to scare me into believing
that my future ain't something worth having belief in,
then trust me, after this poem,
you'll have no choice but to be leaving."

me, flaming and on fire,

I burn holes in the Boogeyman's blindfold, exposing all my
 brilliance.
I am starting to believe that I look like I'm gonna become
my own version of Dwayne Wayne in the different world of
 college life.

I remember how I came out into the world equipped with a puck
 of knowledge,
and if I combine that with Ma's and Tamu's proud cheers,
+ Mr. Marshall's masterful words of wisdom
+ 1 Corinthians 2:9
+ Bubba's and Cubby's encouraging jokes
+ my girl-friends' incantations
+ Blu's love and patience
+ Ebby and Tiffy and Auntye P's fuel

----

then the SAT shall not get the best of me because I understand
 language.

I leave the mirror exactly where it is, undress and climb in my bed,
looking at how bright my light is shining through the
 Boogeyman's dark peeling skin.

SOMETHING POSITIVE

it rained,
but it rained yesterday.
today, sunshine.

the smell of Mother Africa
cooking in my mental stewpot.

the feeling of a church high.

knowing I have a dollar,
which might not be a lot,
but today,
while the sun is shining,
I can buy one glass of my favorite tea,
and sip under the sunshine,
and let my toes tickle in between the grass
still moist from yesterday's shower.

having your smile acknowledged by many faces,
most of whom look like you,
almost a mirror to your own spirit,

because they smile back too.

I think my mom is pondering up my Sunday delicacies,
everything will be sweet,
from the pies to the greens

and today,
I passed an educational assessment,
that means I added another piece of currency
for my future investment.

so, today I am rich.
rich from the feeling of blue-sky kisses
and magic well wishes.

today, I think I'll wish for something positive,
a plus, to override all the negatives:
the deaths,
the diseases,
the heartaches,
depression,
and anything else the media suffocates me with.

because today,
I am listening for those gentle voices
like Whoopi Goldberg in that movie *Sarafina*.
I want gentleness like that.

so, today, I'll be positive.
optimism will be my motivation.
because today I got the best seat
in the house, without making a reservation.

Something Positive

It rained, but it rained yesterday
today sunshine
The smell of Mother Africa cradling in my
~~the~~ mental stew pot
The feeling of a church high
knowing I have a dollar, which may not
be a lot
But today while the sun is shining, I can
buy one glass of ~~my~~ favorite tea
And sip under the sunshine
And let my toes tickle in between the
grass still moist from yesterday's shower

Having your smile acknowledge by many
faces, most of whom look like you.
Almost a mirror to your own ~~happiness~~ spirit
because ~~they smile back~~ they smile
back too.

I think my mom is ~~ponder~~ pondering up
my Sunday delicacies. ~~All~~ Everything
will be sweet, from the pies to the greens
~~And I taste~~
~~I taste~~
and today I passed an educational assessment
that means today I added another piece of
currency for my ~~future~~ future investment
so today I am rich

Rich from the feel of these skie kisses
and ~~remind me~~ magic well wishes
Today I think I'll wish for something
positive
A plus to override all the negatives.
The deaths, the diseases, the ~~heart~~
~~a racked 88~~ heart aches, depression, and
anything else the media suffocates me
with.
Because today I am listening for the
gentle voices like whoopi Goldberg in
that movie Sarafinia, I want to be
taught gentleness like that.

So today I'll be positive, optimism will be
my motivation. Because today I got
~~the~~ best seat in the house, without
making a reservation.

I DREAMT WITHOUT SLEEPING

it's 7:30 a.m.
I levitate off my bed and slam my alarm clock's stop button.
I look at the mirror bouncing back narrow rays of sunlight through
　　the blinds,
and I appear taller than I did the morning before.
I stand up and look at the length of my legs,
convinced that somehow, overnight, I grew upright at least three
　　more inches.

I shower, put on my Old Navy denim staples and my low-cut black
　　Timberland boots,
then I open one of the packs of frosted strawberry Pop-Tarts,
and without toasting the pair of pastries, start to chew and
　　swallow the chalk-powder edges,
leaving the sweet red gelatin-layered oval sandwich to eat on the
　　way out the front door.

I take a short walk across the street to DuVal High,
praying that this third attempt will bring out my good luck charm.

Ms. Peralta is standing at the entrance of the building near the
　　metal detectors

120

next to the main office.

I don't know why DuVal High ain't safe.

I damn sure don't feel fortunate when I am required to wear a
school ID badge,

which *has* to be attached to a cheap plastic white beaded
lanyard

that I must wear, loosely, around my neck,

so that teachers and administrators can identify me based on
my movements

inside of this facility, according to the schedule that they give
me.

Ms. Peralta is our senior-class advisor and has been my Spanish
teacher since sophomore year.

her thin silver and auburn hair is tied in a low ponytail barely
touching the back of her neck.

and she is smiling all the positive energy that I need this morning.

"hola Señor Keith, ¿cómo estás esta mañana?"

I respond, "buenos días, Señora Peralta, me siento bien, gracias.

pero yo soy un poco cansado." then, I pretend to yawn.

she responds firmly, "aht aht aht Señor Keith, yo 'estoy' un poco
cansado."

"oh, that's right!" I say, placing my palm to my face,

disappointed that I forgot how to correctly use the verbs ser and
estar.

I have all As in her class,
but struggle sometimes with translating "how I be"
when speaking a language different from English
that ain't got nothing to do with some kind of standard.

121

Ms. Peralta looks at me proudly and says, "oh, no te preocupes."
Ms. Peralta is from Barcelona, and says that el Español
    she speaks first
is what we are learning in her classroom,
but there are variations of Spanish spoken by people throughout
    Latin America
and in various parts around the world.
I say, "muchísimas gracias," and continue,
"I don't know how to ask you this en Español, pero,
por favor, could you write me a letter of recommendation for
    MSU?"
we are the same height, and so it is easy for her to look into my
    eyes
while wrapping her arm around my right shoulder.
she goes, "por supuesto, mi estudiante favorito, it would be an
    honor."
all of me sinks into her support and I feel less heavy than I did
    before.

then, Ms. Peralta switches codes and passes me a clipboard,
"don't forget that I signed you up to perform one of your poems
at our talent show next Friday."
"I won't. In fact, I've been inspired to write about una enfermedad."
with a confused look on her face she asks, "are you sick, Señor
    Keith?"
I laugh and say, "well, something like that, you'll just have to wait
    and see."
I offer her a smirk that she can't refuse to smile at before she says,

"now, Mr. Keith, can you please sign your name here,
grab a number two pencil, two pieces of scratch paper,
a test booklet, and take the fourth seat at table ten,
we are ready to begin."

I approach the cafeteria and it is silent, sans Black boys tussling
over territories,
and missing student voices competing for volume.
There are three other students here who I don't know,
and they are all facing opposing directions, looking at their feet,
avoiding eye contact with one another.

I don't blame them.
I sit down, close my eyes, and listen to my heart beating for my life,
and I whisper to myself, "buena suerte, Tony."

everything becomes a blur,
or a filled-in bubble,
or an erasure mark,
or a skipped response to a question,
or a chance to make a pattern of the As, Bs, Cs, and Ds
that determine how smart I am.

Three hours and twenty-three minutes later,
I hand Ms. Peralta a paper misrepresentation of my intelligence.
She gives me a wink, as if suggesting that she already knows
that I did my absolute best.

CAN'T CONTROL THE FUTURE

I make the same simple trek back to our apartment and call Aunt
   Tee—Ma's baby sister.
She is too young to be my mother,
and so perhaps it's the short amount of distance in between our
   birth years
that I am more comfortable seeking her guidance
more than I try to troubleshoot life with my mother.
Aunt Tee is more coach than cheerleader,
always reassuring me that I already have answers to a lot of my
   questions,
and that I must celebrate the small victories,
even when the battle ain't won yet.
      She is so wise.

Although she has caller ID, she always picks up right before the
   third ring.
"hey nephew!"
"hey Aunt Tee!"
she always cares deeply about whatever I'm doing
and cuts right to the chase, "so, how'd the test go?"
"not even gonna lie, it's all a blur," I respond.
"but I did feel more confident answering some of the questions

than I did the last two times."

Aunt Tee says, "I'm so happy to hear that you felt better about it
this go-round, nephew."
"thanks, I should have my scores back in a couple of weeks,
right around the time for senior prom."
"oh, that's right!" she exclaims.
"are you and Blu going to each other's proms?"
"yeah, they're on different nights, but we decided to wear the same
    outfits to both events.
I don't see the point in wasting money on buying fancy clothes
that's meant to last *only* for one night,
especially if Pop is the parent making this important purchase."

"I know that's right, nephew!
anyway, what are your plans today?" she asks.
"well, I'm starving like Marvin, so, first up is some food.
we got plenty of stuff in here to cook, but I just don't feel like it.
I'll probably call and ask Cubby for the number to the carryout
that got the bomb wings and fries with mambo sauce.
and if they got a platter special, I'll get a side of shrimp fried rice.
then, I gotta put some words down on my personal statement,
    which could take a while,
and I'll give Blu a call to see what she's up to."

"okay, Mr. Busy Man, well, if you want some *real* food,
I made blackened salmon, Cajun rice, and garlic green beans last
    night,
and there's some leftovers in my fridge that Jay doesn't want

and I've had way more than enough."
I start salivating through the phone, and yell out, "say less!"

I speed walk for three minutes and arrive at Aunt Tee's apartment.
I throw her delicious day-old delicacies down into my grumbling
    belly,
and play several rounds of freeze tag with my little cousin Jay,
        who is exceptional at running quickly
            before becoming completely quiet and remaining absolutely
                still.

as my coach, Aunt Tee always knows how to listen deeply enough
to hear what I'm actually saying behind the words,
and helping me pinpoint the places in my wrinkly brain
where my thoughts get all tangled up.
she'll ask me simple-ass questions that make me ramble on and on
until whatever the thing is that is blocking my freedom
finally figures out a way to get itself   unstuck.

I plop down on her sofa and take a deep breath.
Aunt Tee has burnt umber eyes,
and long, thick black hair, with blond and copper highlights
that she is sweeping to the right side of her honey pecan face,
as she turns the volume down on the television remote.
she asks, "so, nephew, tell me about this personal statement.
how can I help?"

I respond to her question with one exhale of air from my lungs,
"I don't know what to write down that would set me apart

from all the other kids who are also tryna get into college
one second before the buzzer sounds.
I need to set myself apart from them somehow."

"I mean, nephew, it is *your* personal statement,
so, who is the best author of *your* words?"
"well, I am."
"*okay*, so, why don't you know what to write down?" she asks.
"I think it's because I'm still afraid that my application
won't be good enough to get me in anyway."
"so, you're afraid that your application won't be good?"
"yeah, that's what I just said."

her follow-up question slaps me in the face,
"or are you afraid that it is *you*, nephew,
who for some reason ain't good enough to submit the application?"

                        the Boogeyman all up in my ear   screaming.

"nah, I think I'm good, like, at my core and all that, but . . ."
        I search for an answer somewhere inside of words that I can't
                seem to
        be able to express out loud,
                which means coach Aunt Tee has pinpointed the place where
                I am all bounded up.

I hit a roadblock. she knows, and continues,
"with sight unseen, what is your connection to MSU?
how can you express that in your personal statement?"

"you and these questions, ugh," I respond with a smirk.

"I know, it's what I do," she says with a loving smile.
"nephew, look, *you* are the only one with the power and agency
to discover language that will solve those riddles,
you just can't be afraid to figure them out."

I GOTTA FIGURE THIS OUT.

I walk home carrying a slice of Aunt Tee's chocolate cheesecake
wondering about the main point I want the MSU admissions
    officers to know about me
through the picture I am painting of myself in my personal
    statement.

I sit at our family's PC with my fingertips a few centimeters above
    the keys
and I imagine that MSU has launched a satellite into outer space
with technology that would identify who their applicants are based
    on some kind of
sonar locating device that detects how bright each of us appear
    from the ground.

I think about who some of those other last-minute candidates are.
    if any of them are poor, first-generation, possibly gay, Black
        boys
        with a single mother always on the move, and an absent and
            addicted father.
            if any of them sing tenor and write poems to manage
                their emotions.

I zoom myself out and type:

Dear MSU,

The year is 1999, and there are over 270,000,000 people living
in the US; 6,000 of us are twelfth-grade Black kids enrolled in
PG public schools. I represent one of about 300 of those seniors
graduating from DuVal High, where I am recognized by my
teachers, administrators, and classmates as a talented and gifted
learner, and an active student leader who loves language, poetry,
and Black history.

I am also the only member of my immediate family to be within
arm's reach of a college education: an honor, not a burden, and so,
I proudly submit this application for admission to MSU because of
your 130+-year legacy as an HBCU.

I know that your primary mission is the education of Black
Americans, and I am in search of higher learning. I am ready to
extend what I know beyond the twelve years of required school.
I want access and understanding of the knowledge sitting up on
shelves inside of ivory towers, where professors will: teach me
more about myself, personally; inspire me to pursue my passions;
encourage me to chase my dreams; challenge my intellectual
boundaries; support my academic curiosities; push and pull me
forward to the future.

While at MSU, I plan to discover more about myself,
professionally, by majoring in business and exploring careers in
marketing, accounting, leadership, management, and sales to

complement my experience working in retail and customer service.

I am excited to join several of your student clubs and academic honor societies, participate in homecoming games and parades, and possibly pursue membership in one of the nine historically Black Greek-letter organizations on campus.

Lastly, as a blossoming poet, I wish to learn how to express my written and spoken voice in such a way that it remains absolutely true to who I am, but also is loud and strong enough to be heard on both the page and the stage.

I know that MSU offers all the above and so, I would be extremely grateful to receive your acceptance. I promise, I'll be a stellar scholar.

Peace,

Anthony R. Keith Jr.

MY STATEMENT *IS* OFFICIALLY PERSONAL

I head to my room to call and see what Blu is doing.
"hello Ms. Irene, this is Tony, how are you?"
"hey son, I'm doing just fine, sitting here laughing at
      Mr. Anthony,
who is fussing at Blu because she is asking *us* to buy *her*
an outrageously expensive prom dress."
I swear their family are real-life versions of the Huxtables from
      The Cosby Show.

I can hear Blu in the background screaming, "but it'll be really
      cute on me though!"
Mr. Anthony says, with hilarious authority,
"and what job are *you* working that's going to pay me back for it?"
Blu replies to her stepfather, "but, why I gotta pay you back?"
he responds, "ain't nothing in life free,
you're about to go to college, which means you're an adult,
so, you're officially on your own now.
your mother and I are tired of taking care of all you ungrateful,
knucklehead-ass kids who *always* want something,
but don't know the value of real hard work.

"now, you *could* learn a lesson from your boyfriend.

one thing about that Tony is, that boy *always* got himself a job.
and that is the *only* reason why he's always allowed to come in my
    house
and eat up all my food in the first place.

hey there, Tony!" he yells.
"what's up, Mr. Anthony?" I say into the phone,
as if he can both see my smile and hear my response from the
    other side.
Ms. Irene says to me, "don't pay them two silly people any mind.
hold on, here's Blu."

there is a ruffle duffle, a few seconds
before I hear Blu's voice asking, "what's shaking, bacon?"
I respond, "chilling like a villain, floating on top of the ceiling
    while popping penicillin."
we both laugh.

"how'd the test go?" she asks.
"I'm feeling pretty positive about it, plus, I just finished my
    personal statement."
"aw shucks now, let me see your wallet,
because it must have 'bad mama jama' written on the front of it!"
we both giggle with a love jones in our bones.

"what are you up to tonight?" I ask.
"well, Tiffy and I are going to Friendly's for ice cream with L'Jei
    and Trey.
apparently, Trey has something important that he wants to tell us.

do you want to come?" she asks.

"oh yeah, I'm down.

Ma and Tamu are out, but they should get back with the car soon.

the moment they arrive, I'll fly out the door,

and be on my way to meet y'all."

"okay, just make sure to drive safely," Blu says.

"I always do, babe."

"mmmmm-hhhmmm," she responds.

"see you soon," I say.

"alright, bet."

Blu has been worried about my driving ever since I got my license
    junior year,

and accidently swerved Ma's car out of the wrong lane,

and was side-struck way out of boundary by a car driven by an
    uninsured man.

    neither of us were hurt,

    but Ma's car was pretty banged up,

      and apparently the costs of repair made her insurance
        premium climb steeper

    than the value of her automobile.

I'M SAFE ON ARRIVAL

I make sure to coast at 55 miles per hour with my seat belt buckled
    tight,
and mirrors adjusted just right
and pull up to the restaurant in under forty-five minutes.
I walk inside of the diner and Blu's sitting at a booth with the
    crew,
and they're all taking spoonfuls of sky-high scooped vanilla ice
    cream
stuffed inside of a thick mug overflowing with chocolate syrup,
rainbow sprinkles, and red maraschino cherries.

"sorry I'm late, y'all," I say, while sliding on the edge of the seat,
wrapping my arm around my girlfriend,
and catching a whiff from her perfume that smells like
a rich bouquet of fresh flowers right after the rain.

Tiffy is sitting next to L'Jei, a petite cinnamon skin girl
who walks with a slight slant in her leg
because the cancer has been eating parts of it away since she was a
    child.

they are flanked to the left of Trey,
who has dyed the tips of his wheat, shoulder-length locs
into the same color as Tiffy's glass of sweetened strawberry
     lemonade.

"hey Tony!" they all say in unison,
while blinking their bright smiles right back at me.
Blu applies her full primrose pink lips gently to mine,
and places her left hand on my right leg,
then says to me, with air quotes, "you arrived at the perfect time.
Trey was just about to give us 'the' update he's been holding out
     on."

this is my third time hanging around Trey,
and although he is a bit quirky, his energy is always bright and
     colorful,
                              which is also what many people say
                                   when they are describing me.
"oh, cool, well, what is it, Trey?" I ask.

"I'm gay," he says, without a single gasp of hesitation, or infraction
     on his face.
instead, he picks up his spoon and catches a dollop of their shared
mostly melted milkshake dripping down the mug,
and starts slurping the sweet, thawed, and stirred ice cream up
through his narrow lips.
Tiffy and L'Jei squeeze their arms around Trey,
causing his face to warm up on the outside,
while Blu gets up to join the comfort circle.

136

there's a belt tightening around my waist
I blink. I catch. I stop breathing.

Trey tells us about the current battle with his parents after they
    found out
he was secretly chatting with anonymous gay men on the internet,
and looking at photos of their nude physiques,
and watching studio-filmed video productions of men getting
    busy.
                                  I have so many questions
                                      but I ain't sayin' shit.
                              I can already see the Boogeyman
                        trying to make Itself reflect on the shiny
                  silver napkin holder sitting right in front of me.
Trey goes on to tell us the story of how
he came to be one hundred percent sure that he is, indeed, gay,
and makes it clear that he *only* messes with other gay men
because straight boys who get busy with other men are confusing
and require a lot of work.
                              I am trying to listen deeply enough
                                to learn something about myself,
                          sans blue ink pen or yellow notepad.
Trey says, "my sexuality is like a compass.
I've been trying to point myself toward the direction where
people are walking on a straight line,
but my internal arrow just does not naturally *go that way*.
I was unhappy pretending to be comfortable following fictitious
    instructions for my life
that came from some artificial script."

I do not show any emotion.
I am presumably the only straight boy here,
and while I am not Blu's playground bully boyfriend,
I feel like I gotta maintain my masculine presence
or I risk dropping my own compass,
causing a catastrophic loss of my personal sense of geography.

"what do you mean, 'script'?" Blu asks with an intensity in her eyes
that I've never seen in her before.
Trey says we are all bombarded with language in books and music,
and newspaper headlines, and television commercials, and
    magazine advertisements
that say the only way for *any of us* to be is straight.

I KNOW THIS SCRIPT ALL TOO WELL.

truth is, I feel obligated to act out a prescriptive performance every
    day.
some figurative rite of passage into manhood:

first, I gotta find a Christian girl, carry her books at school,
take her to play miniature golf and be a gentleman when I'm
    around her parents.
then, on prom night, we will decide it's time to flex our Get Out
    of Hell Free hall passes,
and pray that we will avoid feeling guilty about getting busy before
    marriage.

after high school graduation,
we will decide to attend separate colleges and officially break up
because a long-distance relationship will not work.
and, while I am breezing my way through higher education,
I will get busy with a bunch of women who are not supposed to be
    as free as me with their bodies.
                    and some of us will say "no," but
                         according to the script,
                   I can ignore the meaning of consent

to touch any of our private parts,
because they intentionally wear their shirts and skirts too short for
my comfort.

which is both gross and really fucked up.

eventually I will find that *special* girl who I won't be able to stop
thinking about,
and who I'll become an absolute fool for
and then we'll start making love.

next thing you know, we're meeting each other's lifelong friends
and attending holiday dinners with each other's families.
and all of them will already hear wedding bells ringing.

and it's only a matter of time before we're college graduates,
living in a tiny apartment, working full-time jobs, saving money to
buy a home,
and paying tithes to a church every single Sunday morning.

and as a straight man of God providing and presiding over our
household,
it will then be my job to propose to my girlfriend with an
expensive diamond ring.
and she will of course say "yes."

and then, my fiancée and I will get married in one of our families'
churches,
followed by an reception that feeds one hundred fifty guests.

because my in-laws will have paid whatever it takes
for *their* daughter to be a blushing bride on our wedding day.

next, we will be newlyweds, spending our honeymoon in the
    Caribbean,
sipping fruity drinks with umbrella straws sticking out of hollow
    coconuts,
lying in turquoise beach chairs with our footsteps sunken deep
    into white sands,
leading us to the tip of clear blue Atlantic Ocean.

and we'll get busy like husbands and wives do on our king-size
    mattress
inside of our new house complete with an asphalt driveway and
    white picket fence.

and after a year or so of marital bliss, my wife will give birth to
    our first child.
and we'll be super excited if it's a healthy baby boy.
and we'll both be confident in knowing that our little bundle of
    joy
and all of our future children will be straight too.

WE ARE PLAYING OUR ROLES PERFECTLY.

after splitting the check, Blu told me that she was proud of Trey
because it's not easy for anyone to come out,
especially a Black boy in America.
she said it takes a lot of guts.
I nodded my head and told her that I could only imagine.
                    and I was indeed imagining what Trey felt like
                        when he spoke about being gay, out loud,
            in a place where folks eavesdrop and spread rumors.
                                        how brave of him.
we embraced for a bit and agreed to see each other at church
    tomorrow.

and I've been awake in bed for hours thinking about Trey
being the first gay person that I've ever met.
although, he probably ain't the only one that I know:
there's been gossip going down the family grapevine for years
about my uncle UT, Ma's oldest sibling,
        the only boy amongst four sisters,
and how he contracted HIV a few years ago
and died of complications from AIDS before his fortieth birthday.

I have memories of UT being   soft.

there was something about his barely five-foot frame
and fresh-faced laughter that was more like a giggle than a true
    chuckle,
that always drew me toward his energy.
his voice was light and airy and whispered in the wind
whenever he spoke about his adventures traveling around the country
with just a bag and a dream.

there are pictures of UT inside of Grandma's photo albums
that prove before he became barely one hundred pounds soaking
    wet,
he was a sturdy, petite, well-dressed, and incredibly handsome
    man
who wore a size six-and-a-half shoe and a gold hoop earring on
    the left side.
he brought bundles of joy everywhere.

but there's one particular photograph living underneath my eyelids
that I can't seem to forget:
one slightly faded Polaroid picture of UT standing side by side
next to a taller and thinner man with cornmeal skin,
a high round shiny brown afro
and a thin and clean chin-strap beard.
he is someone the family only refers to as UT's "friend" Joe.
UT and Joe seem very happy together,
because they are smiling with all their might,
while being closely connected to each other's hips and shoulders
    like *that*.

I saw UT for the last time during ninth grade
at the hospital, where he'd been for several days:

his torso perched up
his arms connected to tubes with clear fluids dripping down into a
    plastic bag,
his legs stretched out on a foam-padded table with sterile white
    sheets,
and umpteen bottles of medication forming a backdrop behind his
    bed,
in the private section of the intensive care unit.

his maple skin was not shiny.
his beard was not full and fluffy either.
his bald head wasn't as smooth as glass.
he was moving ever so slowly,
as if everything inside of him was breaking apart into tiny pieces
and flying around in circles,
tearing up whatever strength was left inside
whichever organs remained intact enough to keep him alive.

my uncle's body ate itself to death
and it did so in small bites.

I tried hard not to cry.
                    I wondered how he got sick like that,
            and if he was gay, would I suffer the same fate?
                and whether Joe was at UT's funeral

watching me cry into my mother's chest
when her brother's casket was lowered six feet in the ground
for as long as forever is forever.

I wondered if Joe was crying too
and if he was, who held him.

WE WERE BOYS ALL DEEP IN OUR FEELINGS.

I wonder what UT would've told me,
if I told him what happened just a few weeks before he died:

Ma moved us to Silver Spring, MD, to help Grandma care for
    him,
which meant Tamu and I had to attend Kennedy High:
        some prestigious public school made up of mostly white folks
            with a swimming pool, tennis court, and fields for golf,
                football, soccer, and lacrosse.
the athletes had a private locker room behind the gymnasium,
where I saw the Boogeyman on the day I tried out for the track
    team:

it was my first year of high school,
and although I'm scared to play sports with playground bully
    boys,
I felt like I needed to be running somewhere.
but I am unprepared for the first practice.
I didn't have a second set of secondhand clothes that would make
    me less heavy
to run the two-mile circumference of Kennedy's perimeter.

I was wearing baggy passed-down, light blue denim jeans,
an extra-long, short-sleeved, red-and-green-striped polo shirt,
and black and white low-top Nikes with the tongue hanging out
that Cubby let me borrow   for a long term.

I tried keeping pace with the other boys,
dressed appropriately in shorts that grant their legs enough space
      to move,
and plenty of room to breathe in between each one of their long
      strides.

I didn't run fast.
I didn't run slow.
I found some cadence in the middle.

forty-five minutes later, we were all sitting on benches inside of
      the locker room,
catching our breath after stretching our limbs over the top of one
      another
on the hard and cold gymnasium floor.

            the place smelled like one thousand gallons of Darin's scent
                  were simmering in a stewpot with the lid off.

I sat silently, keeping my head low   remaining calm.
I figured if I just breathed slow enough, my internal temperature
      would cool down,
and my outfit would dry itself out enough to not look so droopy.

I didn't plan to make a peep until I heard someone ask out loud,
"yo, freshman, where are you from?"

I immediately recognized it was Eric's voice.
  he was a popular and handsome Black sophomore
   that looks like someone with parents who have filled their
    entire house
   with trophies that honor their son's outstanding athleticism.
   we've never looked in each other's directions, at least not on
    purpose,
   let alone have we parted lips to acknowledge our collective
    humanity.

I slowly tilted my hot head upward toward Eric's cool direction,
and his honey pecan eyes were staring directly into my translucent
  skull.
I am surprised to confirm that he is, indeed, speaking to me
while standing at his locker four spaces down on the left on the
  bottom row.

I see that not only has he taken his soaking wet white T-shirt off,
exposing his bare walnut chest and semihairy belly
with two and a half front abdominal muscles,
but his shorts are draped loosely around the top of his knees.
and he is using his right hand to reach inside of his boxer briefs to
  adjust his private parts, I guess,
   to ensure everything is sitting where it should comfortably
   after exhausting all that energy running directly in front of
    me.

148

I should not be looking at Eric like *this*.

what am I, a sissy or something?

I quickly shift my gaze toward my locker where I ain't got shit,
and I see the Boogeyman staring at me through my reflection in
    the mirror.
I can't tell whether I am It   or It is me.

this ain't blind man's bluff.

he asked again, "yo, freshman, you hear me talking to you?"
I blink. I catch. I stop breathing.

I speak to Eric with the same volume that he is using
to cut through the tense stench filling up this locker room.
"oh, my bad, um, yeah, you asked me where I'm from?"
"yeah, do I need to come closer for you to hear me better?"

yes.

"no, you're good.
I'm from DC but I moved to Montgomery County a few months
    ago
after living in PG for a lil while."
Eric rotates his head and lifts his ears like a dog deciphering
    human language
and says, "that sounds complicated," followed by a laugh that I
    enjoy watching.

I am burning up and terrified.

"yeah, it's a little something like that," I respond,
looking down at my heirloom sneakers
    their tongues are stretched out dragging across the floor,
    sliding on the condensation falling down the concrete walls

and dripping off the ceiling.
Eric continues his benevolent questioning,
"so, freshman, are you serious about running for Kennedy?
not to be a jerk, but you didn't look like you're enjoying yourself
    out there."

whole time, I'm trying to figure out how in the hell it's possible
    that Eric and I are having a clear-ass one-on-one conversation
            amongst this musky atmosphere of masculinity,
                with other boys who seem to be comfortable
        chatting half-naked, standing up close with one another and
                    feeling fully free.

I respond, "I don't think I'll be able to join the team.
I'm supposed to be getting a job soon, so I probably won't be able
    to stay for practice."
I lie, "showing up today was a spur-of-the-moment decision,
hence, I didn't bring any of my gym clothes."

"oh yeah?" he asks, suspiciously.
"where are you going to work?"
"anywhere that will hire me," I say.

"I see," he says, while squinting his eyes at me as if the halo above
    his crown of cornrows
isn't shining all its light directly into his cognac corneas.
                            keep breathing, Tony.
"well, perhaps you should check out Homecrest House,

150

they're always hiring Kennedy students."
"oh okay, I'll be sure to check them out."

then, while still drenched myself,
I slide my book bag on my right shoulder,
slam the locker and exit my purgatory   stage left
without uttering another word to Eric for the duration of the
    school year.

I didn't even wait to see if he would've asked me my name.

BEING OUT IS RISKY

I prayed for Trey on my way to church this morning,
asking God to keep him safe from harm while he figures out his
    way
in a world that doesn't want him: me: us: we to win.

I don't often follow the biblical stories that Pastor Jenkins be
    preaching about.
I only read the scriptures listed on the program during the order of
    service
when we are required to call and respond with whoever is
    speaking on the microphone
in the pulpit or to either side of the altar.
I just look forward to this part when Kirk instructs the musicians
to play a melody that is in sync with Pastor Jenkins's rhythmic
    speech,
because I know something otherworldly is destined to happen.

our spiritual leader has taken off his gold watch and unloosened
    his white collar
just enough to keep it tight around his neck.
his long sepia arms are shooting out from underneath the bell

152

sleeves on his grape robe
and he is pressing his hands down firmly on the sides of the
  wooden podium,
    hollering into the microphone and across the atmosphere,
      as if proving how preaching is an art for moving a
        congregation.
      as if rapper, poet, emcee, and preacher all got something
        in common.
        'cause I swear they all be speaking words for an
          audience
        that be inspiring all our bodies to be free enough
        to feel the vibrations bouncing around inside some
          sacred cipher.

I see the back of Pastor Jenkins's head from the choir stand,
and so, from my perspective, he is quite literally at the center of us
  and the musicians,
and every single person on the floor and up in the balcony,
  all of whom are directly facing right in front of me.

Pastor Jenkins says, "some of you try to hide in the light,
you believe that you have the power to escape how much
the sun loves to shine itself on top of your Black skin.
you are convinced that almighty God,
the one who created all that we know within this world and
  beyond it,
wants you to avoid basking in a glow
raining down from the same heaven that He specifically designed

for us to be together
in the here and now, and the life after.

"who? I ask you, who *exactly* do you think you are?"

He wonders if there are any witnesses in here,
as if he can't see that most of us are standing up on top of each
    other's feet,
with our hands reached out toward him.
        as if we are trying to grab hold of the two parts of hydrogen
        and one part of oxygen atoms that are spitting out from his
            mouth,
        and flooding the sanctuary with holy water up to our knees.

            "c'mon here, preacha!" shouts the Amen corner.

"I'll tell you who, because some of y'all don't want to realize this
    for yourselves.
I'mma, I'mma, I'mma, I'mma help some of y'all out this morning!
is that alright with you?"
                they respond again, "help us, Lord!"

"who, who, who, who in here need some assistance?"
                                            me.
"who needs to be delivered from a belief that they are undeserving
    of agape love?"
                                            me.
"who wants to feel what it's like to burn bright from the fire of the

Holy Ghost?"

                                                                        me.

                        the Amen corner goes, "oh hallelujah, Jesus!"

then, the drummer taps his foot on the bass every ten seconds,
and Kirk starts playing a tune on the keyboard that sounds like
    "bah doom doom doom doom."
suddenly, Pastor Jenkins sets his Bible down and pulls a handkerchief
    from his pocket
wiping off sweat falling from his forehead and down the back of
    his neck.
he starts inhaling and exhaling his extemporaneous words
by drawing long and hard breaths in between his calls to us,
        as if trying to sustain our responses according to some divine
        cadence.

"God is telling *me* that there is one of *you* who believes that you
    are the Boogeyman."

                                                                        me.

"you think that you're ugly, uhhhhhhhh ahhhhhh!"

                                                                        yes.

"you think that you're scary, uhhhhhhhh ahhhhhh!"

                                                                        yes.

"you think that you're some kind of terrifying sight for sore eyes
who can only exist as a shadow in the darkness, uhhhhhhhh
    ahhhhhh!"

                                                                        yes.

"and you think it's your fault, uhhhhhhhh ahhhhhh!"

                                                                yes.

"you think that God is punishing you, uhhhhhhhh ahhhhhh!"

                                                                yes.

"you think that He don't love you, uhhhhhhhh ahhhhhh!"

                                                                yes.

"but, my brothas and sistas, I came here to tell you today
that yyyyooouuuu are a reflection of Himmmmmm, uhhhhhhhh
        ahhhhhh!
which meeeeeaaaaannnnns that the real problem issssssss
that yyyyooouuuu don't love yourself when you look in the mirror,
        uhhhhhhhh ahhhhhh!"

                                the Amen corner goes, "gloraaaay!!!!"

"but I am here to remind you that you are alllllllll worthy to receive
        His divine blessings,
and you ain't got to be scared no more!
now, give God some praise up in here!"
we are all clapping our hands.

                "thank ya, Lord!" they shout out with fast footwork and
                                                flailing arms.

then, Kirk settles the drums and makes subtle keystrokes
emanating a calm and serious song without any words.
Yolanda asks us to hum our own melodies   softly to
        ourselves,
creating an unwritten harmony of celestial noise.

then, Pastor Jenkins says, with a gentle and relaxed tone,
"if you are not sure whether you deserve to stand inside of His
    light,
I want you to come down to the altar from wherever you are,
so that we can all pray for you."

                    I don't remember walking to join this multitude of people
                            gathered near Pastor Jenkins's feet,
                    and I can't seem to open my eyes without salt water
                                        gushing out of them.
            I can feel someone's warm hand pressed against my forehead,
            and they are speaking in a tongue that ain't got nothing to do
                                        with English.

Pastor Jenkins tells us at least five times that we've been delivered.
then, he asks us all to return our brand-new selves
back to where the undelivered one migrated from.
I walk back to the choir stand and look up at Blu, who is in a deep
    prayer of her own.

I wonder whether God finally performed a miracle
by making me believe that I should have no reasonable doubts
that I am one hundred percent straight.

NOW THAT I AM DELIVERED

I wait until 10:43 p.m. to test out my sexual compass
and tiptoe into our dining room and power on our family's PC.
Ma is asleep and Tamu just left to go to a DC nightclub.

I pull out the soft plastic sleeve with "AOL Instant Messenger
    (AIM)" written on it.
I slide the disk out from its protective armour and insert it in the
    slot
suddenly, the machine starts screaming for its entire life,
as if whatever AIM is doing to it is stretching its wires beyond
    their capacity,
causing excruciating pain to the electrical parts of its kidneys.
I am sitting in front of a fax machine sending a message into
    space,
        using Morse code dashes that shoot out like wailing warnings
        of a banshee.
after a few seconds of panicking about all the noise I'm making in
    the matrix,
all the loud weeping becomes a calming hum.

I look at the monitor, and I am met with a blue screen

that has a cartoon picture of a yellow person moving stage right, in
    a hurry.
and they are asking me if I am ready to set up my "username."
I think about who I am and type "tonydapoet" into the text box.

I am then prompted to enter the number of a major credit or debit
    card
to start my seven-day trial, which will become $19.95 every
    month.
I reach in my right back pocket and retrieve my wallet.
    one of UT's heirlooms
      came complete with a crispy one-dollar bill inside
        I wrote "Do not spend!!! Lucky dollar!!" on it.
        now, I always, at least, got a dollar to my name.

I have $78.04 in my checking account and $25.06 in savings,
and it's seven days before I get paid again.
I make a mental note, reminding myself to call the 1-800 number
    to cancel my subscription
I press "confirm," and my screen splits into four different sections.

the first section is telling me the local weather is 66 degrees.
the second one is displaying a headline: "Columbine High School
    Massacre."
the third section is informing me that I have two unread emails in
    my inbox.
the last section is inviting me to join a virtual chat room space,
where anonymously, people around the world with similar interests

are discussing their commonalities on the "world wide web"
which I hope ain't got no sticky boundaries I'mma have to fight
    for.

within two clicks of searching the keyword "gay men,"
I see a chat room called Curiously Gay Guys.
I select Enter and the next screen asks if I am at least eighteen.
I look over my shoulder to confirm that God would be the only
    witness to my lie,
        just one year before it's true.
and plus I'm delivered, so I don't anticipate any additional divine
    interventions.
I have no idea what will happen, but I confirm that I am indeed,
ready to experience messaging whoever from wherever they are.

within a few seconds, I find myself inside of a digital world
where strangers are chatting in shorthand, using terms like "lol,"
    "a/s/l," "brb."
I type: "how do you know if you're gay?"
it takes about three seconds for my message to rise and disappear
amongst the collective chatter.
I wait for something to happen,
but all I see is other people engaged in a deep discussion
about safe ways gay folks get busy: silicone vs. water-based
    lubricants,
the proper usage of condoms for reducing your risk of HIV
    exposure.

there are people with taglines that say things like "top," "bottom,"
    "versatile,"
"jock," "bear," "twink," "leather," "chaser" . . .
        none of which make any sense to me.
I try to keep up with the conversations
but there are far too many individuals and symbols
swinging around in this jungle of screen names,

then, a tiny window pops up that says "itsok2bu" is inviting me to
    a private chat.

I ACCEPT.

itsok2bu: hello there. believe it or not, we get your question quite a bit in this chat room, and the answer is always different for everybody.

tonydapoet: wow, I thought I was alone.

itsok2bu: nope, you are one star in a galaxy full of human beings who all just want to be unconditionally loved by everybody else.

tonydapoet: so, how will I know?

itsok2bu: first, my name is Kyle. I run a small non-profit with Pete, my partner for the last twenty years. we provide emergency resource housing for gay and queer boys and young men in Baltimore, MD.

tonydapoet: oh, that's dope! I didn't know people could have jobs like that.

itsok2bu: absolutely, although they don't pay very well. we rely mostly on donations but have gotten a few grants to keep us afloat.

tonydapoet: wow. where do the people who stay with you come from?

itsok2bu: most of them are fleeing from homes where they don't feel safe enough to be themselves and they are afraid of harm.

tonydapoet: yeah, I know someone who recently came out as gay and his parents are practically disowning him right before he goes away to college.

itsok2bu: oh, that's terrible to hear.

itsok2bu: Pete and I created this virtual safe space to keep in touch with the kids who briefly stay with us before returning to their families. but a few months ago, they requested that we allow other people to join the chat who might need help too.

itsok2bu: and, while we don't censor anything, we do mine the chat room for the presence of predators, and remove any comments that are meant to hurt any of us.

tonydapoet: so, does being here mean that I'm gay?

itsok2bu: I don't think it's that simple lol but, if anything, it might suggest that you're at least curious about your sexuality.

itsok2bu: and there's nothing wrong with wanting to understand yourself and the world around you, especially when things aren't quite making sense.

tonydapoet: I mean, I've never gotten busy with another guy before and although I have a girlfriend, we're both virgins.

tonydapoet: and I don't quite understand how gay men determine the ways in which their bodies will fit together.

itsok2bu: just take your time and when the right moment comes along, you'll discover the answer to your question.

tonydapoet: thanks, Kyle.

itsok2bu: np. so, is it safe to assume that your name is "Tony," and you're a "poet"?

tonydapoet: yeah, I guess I made that pretty obvious, huh?

itsok2bu: a little bit lol so, what is your poetry about?

tonydapoet: I usually write poems to express how I'm feeling, but I don't share many of those with anyone except my girlfriend.

tonydapoet: I'll also write poetry for friends just to make them smile. although, I charge between $1.00 to $5.00 for creating custom pieces for people.

tonydapoet: I made $15 on Valentine's Day after writing love poems for my friends to give to their crushes.

itsok2bu: now, that sounds like a cool job to have!

tonydapoet: I'm more like a starving artist hahaha! I've never met any Black men who are full-time poets or writers.

itsok2bu: well, I'm a white guy, and I know how many of us are authors, but have you ever read anything written by Langston Hughes, Countee Cullen, Claude McKay, or James Baldwin?

tonydapoet: actually, I have! my girlfriend gifted me an anthology of Black poetry for my birthday last year and it has some of their work.

tonydapoet: one of my favorites is "Motto" by Langston Hughes

itsok2bu: that's a cool poem! but, did you know that not a single one of those well-known Black authors were straight?

tonydapoet: what? really?

itsok2bu: yup. there are quite a few Black gay and queer writers from the Harlem Renaissance. Pete and I keep a lot of their books in our home so the kids can read stuff that was written by people who were just like them.

tonydapoet: wow. I wonder if my poetry has anything to do with me being gay or not?

itsok2bu: and yet another really great question. you're on a roll tonight, Tony!

tonydapoet: my aunt always says that I already have the answers somewhere inside me.

itsok2bu: then I think she would say that you have quite the riddle to solve lol

tonydapoet: yeah, I suppose I do.

itsok2bu: so, how do you feel about talking to your family about all this?

tonydapoet: I'd rather know for sure before I tell them anything, because they can all be a little overdramatic sometimes.

itsok2bu: lol aren't they all.

itsok2bu: well, Tony, I'm going to log out for the night and get ready for work in the morning, but feel free to hang out in the chat room as long as you need.

itsok2bu: add me as a friend, and if you see me online be sure to say hello, ok?

tonydapoet: ok, will do, and thanks for all your help.

itsok2bu: you bet.

itsok2bu: signed off

tonydapoet: signed off

I CANCELED MY SUBSCRIPTION

I couldn't afford to keep going down internet rabbit holes about
    gay people,
but I saw for the first time all the things Trey was talking about.
and I understand what he meant about how he feels about himself
and the ways in which men fit themselves together for love,
    pleasure, and protection.

I too wanted to get busy like them,
but the Boogeyman kept reminding me that our family PC ain't
    private
and I didn't want Ma to do to me
what Trey's parents are doing to him.
    let alone, let Pop find out.
I learned how to clear my browsing history from the chat room,
and now I just remain logged out.

instead I spent my nights writing this poem for the talent show
    today.
all exhausted and anxious, I couldn't stop thinking about the
    concept of time:
        how long would it be before I fell asleep?

167

where in Earth's orbit is the moon?
how soon will my side of the planet rotate in front of the
    sun?
how many weeks left before I start adulting?
how old will I be before I kiss another Black boy?
    when will Blu find out about me?
when will I feel free?

and so, I wrote a piece that tries to connect the dots between
now and graduation day.
I don't know if everyone will understand it,
but I know there's at least one person who can relate.

our host, Catriba, the tallest girl at DuVal, just thanked Ms.
    Peralta
for helping us make it to the end of senior year,
and is introducing the first act: an all-girl step show team
coached by Ms. Valentino, the art teacher who is a member of a
    Black sorority.

Ms. Peralta walks over and hands me a sealed white envelope
with my recommendation letter snugged up inside.
she says, "here you go, señor Keith, estoy esperando tu poema."
I respond, "gracias, yo también."

Mr. Marshall gave his letter to Ms. Zbornak last week.
I wonder if whatever they wrote about me will matter enough
to convince Mr. Fiasco to let me into MSU.

Catriba goes, "alright, y'all, the next person to come to the stage
is someone who needs no introduction,
after all he is our senior-class poet.
y'all give it up for Tony Keith!"

I love my voice on the microphone
and I ain't scared to be up here staring at the sea of faces with skin
reflecting light on multiple shades of the spectrum staring at me.
this is how it be when I'm singing with GLC's youth choir.
the only difference is, I'm not performing someone else's gospel
    song,
I'm reading an original poem on the stage today.

I walk up and grab the standing microphone while the audience
    claps.
"what's up, everybody?" I ask into the black felt sphere
that is ten centimeters away from touching my top and bottom lip.
"hey Tony!" I hear a few people yell out somewhere, generating a
    mild applause.

                              I think about Pastor Jenkins
                and how he uses his voice to speak out vibrations
                              that gets people in the choir
        and folks in the congregation so excited that we have no choice
            but to stand on our feet and throw words from our mouths
                              toward the sky,
            because to sit still would be an intentional denial of the
                              presence of God.

I raise my volume up by ten decibels and ask again,
"I said, what's up, DuVal High?" except this time,
I imagine that I am looking into the eyes of every single person in
    the room
and that my voice can fly inside of their ears.
this sparks a fire on everyone's fingertips
causing their hands to clap a little harder than before.

                                    just the momentum I need.

"where are all the seniors at?" I ask, which is followed by
    screaming and hollering.
        all of us acting like we ain't got no damn home training.
some folks are literally barking at the first years, sophomores, and
    juniors,
while others are standing up on the chairs
shouting out loud in a call and response with each other:
        "awwww '99!"
        "say what now?"
        "awwww '99!"
        "one more time!"
        "awwww '99!"

I smile hard, knowing that I am not alone in this moment.
"that's what I'm talking about," I respond.
"I love this energy.
alright, so I wrote this poem as a reflection of a typical day as a
    graduating senior."

I unfold the paper stashed inside my right front pocket,
close both my eyes, take a deep breath, open them again
and then read my written poem in its spoken form
while also looking at the audience and taking pauses in between
    lines
and stressing specific words that are intentionally meant to rhyme.

SENIORITIS

tick tick tick goes my heart
as it races with the clock
the seconds are flying
not forward, but rewinding
my feet are tapping on the pale stone tile
my legs are giants as they shade the center aisle
my head is leaned back resting on an oak wood board
my eyes are like daggers, but stabbing like swords

my fingers are lifeless like a neck at a lynching
and faint in the background my ears pause to listen
to hear the grumbling monstrous voice
as it swells to mention
causing me to rise and pay attention

tock, tock, tock goes my mind
as it competes with the time
hours and seconds become infinite labor
and like a dyslexic child my mind organizes the paper

on my neck, I can feel a breath
but not from inside
it's an open window where the leaves play
it's the breeze from outside
my back is glued to this plastic body brace
the look of exhaustion and boredom can be traced
along the wrinkles on my forehead and
the crimson on my face

tap, tap, tap goes the sound
of my foot on the ground
impatience has become
my only acquaintance
although transparent and imaginary
the small sand-drenched man who flies like a fairy
the smell of perspiration and thinking
inside my soul is sinking
the misty chalk commands my eye blinking

throb, throb, throb goes my pulsating brain
the matrixes filled with numbers are used to count my pain
it's a fever beyond 100 degrees
my inferno is singed to the point my thought freezes

can anyone relate to this common virus
that's causing this lethargically feverish crisis?

Senioritis.

I did it.

there are waves forming in a sea of students
who have their arms extended out, clapping in the air,
    as if trying to grab hold of my evaporating H_2O.
I take a slight bow with my hands folded together as if in prayer,
and I say, "thank you, DuVal High!"
then, I exit stage left, before the audience finishes bouncing
    around all the energy
that I put out into the atmosphere.

Tick
Tick
Tick goes my heart - - - -
as it races with the clock - - - -
The seconds are flying ~~more forward~~
Not forward but rewinding - - - - -
My feet are tapping on the pale stone tile - - - -
My legs are giants as the shade the center aisle - - -
My head is leant back resting on an oak wood board - - -
My eyes are like daggers, but stabbing like swords - - -
My fingers are lifless like a neck at a lynching - - -
And faint in the background my ears pause to listen - - -
to hear the grumbling monstrous voice as it swells to mention
Causing me to arise and pay attention - - - -
Tock
Tock
Tock goes my mind - - - -
As it competes with the time - - -
Hours and seconds have become infinitized labor - - -
And like a dislexic child my mind organizes the paper - - -
on my neck, ~~Rear~~ - - -
I can feel a breath - - -
But not from inside - - - -
Its an open window, where the leaves play
Its the breeze from outside - - - -
My back is glued to this plastic body brace - - -
The look of exhaustion, and boredom can be traced - - -
Along the wrinkles on my forehead and the crimson on my face.
Tap
Tap

Tap goes the sound
of my foot to the ground
Impatience ~~has become my~~
has become my only acquaintance
~~Alt~~ Although transparent and imaginary
The small sand drenched man who flys like a fairy
The smell of prespiration and thinking
Inside my soul ~~is sinking~~ it is sinking
The misty chalk commands my eye blinking
Throb
Throb
Throb goes my pulsating brain
The matrixes filled with numbers are used to count my pain
It's a fever ~~too~~ beyond 100° degrees
My inferno is singed to the point, my thought freezes
Can any ~~senior~~ relate to this common virus
Thats causing this lethargically, feverish crises
          Senioritis!

PREACHING POEMS.

I performed at last year's talent show too,
but instead of a poem, I rapped the rock-remixed version of
Puff Daddy's "It's All About the Benjamins" with my friends Lil
    Man, Tevaughn, and Trina.
I remember feeling real cute and extra confident onstage,
rocking my fresh white T-shirt and a pair of black baggy, swishy
    track pants,
a black Versace baseball cap, and a pair of Wayne Gretzky Nikes
        all garments borrowed from Bubba, Cubby, and my buddy
            Alex.

I took the microphone right off the stand after LiL Man did
    Diddy's part,
and I was all deep-boy braggadocio when I spit Jadakiss's bars
about figures, malt liquor, gold diggers, and gold zippers.
I puffed out my chest, drew my face into itself, grabbed my private
    parts,
and commanded all of the space I could take up on the stage.

there was a surge of energy shooting through my entire body,
made me believe I could rock an entire stadium arena full of fans:
        folks screaming for me to move them to call and respond

and lift their hands,
while I sweat and spit and hoop and holla and hum and hah
and throw my voice against the booming speakers
where the bass shakes all of our stiff body parts loose.

perhaps my straightest performance yet.

but I don't think gay boys can become hip-hop music stars.
. . . can't be soft in a solid-gold industry where punk, sissy, faggot,
and bitch
are lyrics that sell out concerts and generate *Billboard* record sales.
perhaps there are rappers with "friends" who they don't
speak about,
but don't mind standing close to.
I wonder if they write poetry to keep away their own
Boogeypeople too.

Gary, one of Tamu's best boy-friends, told me: rap *is* poetry.
he said you just gotta make the poems rhyme,
all while spitting your rhythmic bars on time.
and he would know, as one of DuVal High's most favorite
emcees.
sophomore year, I saw him freestyle for sixteen minutes
about how much he appreciated the cafeteria workers.
he also did two original raps and spit bars between the verses of
Tupac's "Do for Love" with live background vocals.
he graduated last year, but Tamu says he still asks about me.

my first time emceeing at an event was in third grade,

when Tamu and I were a part of a group of Black kids on the Base
who did not attend the same school with some of the white kids
that also lived in our military housing circle.
we were shipped off one and a half miles beyond
our barricaded border around the rest of southeast DC,
to attend McGogney Elementary in Congress Heights in Ward 8.

I was in Ms. Melodie's class when I wrote my first poem called
    "Seasons."
it was about experiencing the changes between summer and fall
while walking in the forest and it began with a simple rhyme:
                    all the leaves on the ground
                    red, yellow, green, and brown . . .

apparently, my poem was so good that Ms. Melodie stapled it to
    the bulletin board
among the rest of my classmates' handwritten works of literary art.
then she asked me to be the master of ceremonies
at our school-wide celebration of Principal Elliot's leadership.
        Ma was so proud, watching me, her baby, stand in the middle
            of the stage
        and without a microphone, lead the program from start to
            finish,
        keeping the audience engaged and informed of all that was
            going down.
            that's when Pop-Pop nicknamed me "Mr. Guest
                Speaker,"
                    he'd say my spoken words are destined to be
                    shared with the world.

I SURE DO LOVE AN AUDIENCE.

I'm getting my prom suit today.
it's been a while since I seen Pop
so I'm excited to see his Jeep parked out front of our apartment.
he is blowing cigarette smoke out through the driver-side window
and unwrapping the foil around a stick of gum.
I smile the exact moment when I see him
because I know that I look like I am created from several parts of
    him.
        it's something about the way skin hangs deep underneath our
            eyes,
        and how our voices vibrate around people when we're being
            serious.

my stepmother Star rolls down the passenger window and yells
    out,
"hey Lil Tony!" with a shimmering gold smile,
forming a foundation of bright light around her hazel eyes and
    smooth tan skin.

"hey Mom," I say, while climbing into the back seat.
I never referred to Pop's second wife with such distinction.

truth is, I didn't get to know her long enough before he and
    Star
were walking down the aisle on their wedding day,
    which Tamu and I actually participated in.
                        Star and Ma remind me of each other.
    perhaps it has something to do with all four of their children
not having the full physical presence of their father in their lives.
                        my stepsiblings Ray and Chét
            never talk about the man involved in creating them,
                and I don't ask them about him either.

Pop's Jeep smells like tobacco, spearmint-flavored Freedent gum,
Drakkar Noir cologne, and Black Ice Tree Air Freshener from the
    car wash.
"what's up, Shorty Bus Stop?" he asks,
while squeezing the back of my head with his right hand,
    still fascinated with my puck full of knowledge.
"Shorty Bus Stop" is one of many nicknames Pop has given me
    over the years,
inspired by the size of my noggin.
        he says that my skull was so damn heavy as a kid
        that a vehicle suitable for transporting dozens of public
            passengers
        could idle itself atop my crown during regularly scheduled
            breaks on its daily route.
"hey, what's up, Pop?" I respond, placing my book bag on the floor
    behind his seat.

our portion of the blended family drive to a K&G's,
where my father's military discount will ensure we get the best
    deal.
Pop tells me all about his new job as a driver for a transportation
    company in DC.
he is proudly rattling off the names of various members of
    Congress who I don't know
that ride around in the back seat of some luxury black vehicle he
    uses
to drive them from point A to points B and C.

it's clear that he wants me to believe that he is doing better
than what he thought was his absolute best many years before,
but without actually saying those exact words.

I don't tell him that I still think about Ma taking me and Tamu to
    see him,
living in a drug rehabilitation facility designed to deliver people
from addiction and damnation through healthy living and
    salvation.

    I was a child when I was escorted by nice people wearing
        uniforms
    into a housing unit to visit with Pop while he was in recovery.
    all I remember is not knowing who he was at first glance,
    but recognized him the moment I heard his voice saying
        something about Star
    being in there with him, but they were restricted from seeing

each other
during this crucial part of the process.

I don't share any of this with them as we ride to the mall
because at this moment, we are together and they are sober,
and that is all that matters.
instead, I just lean forward toward the center of the back seat
with the safety buckle secured around my waist
and listen to Pop not talk about missing traveling around the
world
servicing US military aircraft.

I tell my parents all about my "Senioritis" poem, the SAT,
MSU, FAFSA, and of course, singing with GLC's youth choir.
they are especially proud that I found a church home.
Pop says, "eyes have not seen, nor ears have heard,
nor has it entered the heart of man
the things which God has prepared for you."
"I know, Pop, I know."

"SO, HOW'S SNOWBALL?"

Pop is the king of nicknames, he just assigns them to people based
   on whatever
their spirit makes him think about.
he says that for some reason Blu reminds him of a Guelder-rose,
     also known as a snowball bush because of its dense flower
        clusters
     that resemble hand-rolled mounds of ice crystals
     that grow while suspended in the atmosphere.
     I guess Blu *is* kinda like that, always shape-shifting herself in
       midair.

"she's doing good," I say.
"it looks like we both may have a chance at going to MSU in the
   fall.
If anything, she's probably freaking out about her prom dress."
Pop goes, "I'll be glad when you two get married and give me
   some grandkids."
I blink. I catch. I stop breathing.
"um, I don't know about all that, especially not right now."
"well, why not?" he asks.

                  I'm feeling attacked.

184

"what's the rush?" I respond.

"Blu and I do not need to live out some life that everyone else
      expects for us.

besides, becoming a father is so far away from where I am right
      now,

and where I am trying to be tomorrow.

I just want to move out of Ma's house, go to college, and figure the
      rest of it out as I go."

"well son, if you fail to plan, plan to fail."

                                          I shut down.

"look, I am not planning to be anyone's husband or parent anytime
      soon period."

"Second Corinthians 6:14 says, be ye not unequally yoked . . ."

before Pop could finish sending out the three-point biblical
      response

that he already has prepared for this moment, Star interjects,

"Lil Tony, what color is Blu wearing again?"

she briefly looks at her husband,

as if signaling that it was time for him to pass the baton

before he and I *really* begin racing against each other

in some endless relay of words and wits.

"silver," I respond, agreeing to change the subject

and avoid rolling this snowball farther off some steep cliff.

Pop remains silent and puts the Jeep in park as we pull up to
      K&G's.

Star says, "okay, you need a dark three-piece suit

and a French collar shirt with a tie that will complement her dress
and not distract you from standing out."
I laugh and say, "sounds good to me, Ma."
one thing about my stepmother is, she always knows what to wear.
        I rarely see her in the same outfit twice.

with some slight tension between us and a sartorial strategy in
    mind,
we are in and out of the discount custom clothing retailer
in less than twenty-five minutes,
complete with the perfect multipurpose suit.

Pop drops me off in front of my apartment building.
I pretend as if I don't see him and Star speaking underneath their
    breath,
while digging dollar bills out of their pockets, wallets, and bags.
they pool together $40 in folded cash,
which Pop extends to me from the driver-side window.

"hey son, I don't know if you have any money in your wallet,
but here's a little something just in case you need it."
we always do this ritual of gifts whenever temporarily parting
    ways.
and it's never because I ask for anything,
        I think somewhere in Pop's mind, helping me
        helps him wrestle with his whereabouts when I was a child
            version of him.

186

I tell my parents that I love them and look forward to seeing them
at my prom night send-off next Friday.

Pop blurts out, "Shorty Bus Stop, how are y'all getting to prom?"
"oh, I was planning to drive Ma's car."
"nah son, you don't have to do that.
let me take care of it for you.
I'll arrange for a long black limousine to pick you up and carry you
    both back.
how does that sound?"
Star looks at Pop with her left eyebrow raised and right brow
    lowered,
but she doesn't say anything.

I respond excitedly, "word, are you serious, Pop?
oh my God, that would be amazing!"

"of course, my son, anything for you."

I'VE GOT BUTTERFLIES IN MY BELLY

it's the evening of my senior prom and I'm standing in our living
    room
with my left arm extended out toward Ma's right hand,
and she is carefully lacing steel cuff links through slots at the
    bottom of my white cuffs.
Tamu has my Polaroid camera and is snapping instant
    photographs,
documenting all my formal preparation.

I am wearing a midnight blue polyester-cotton blend
three-piece suit with silver vertical pinstripes,
along with the matching button-down vest Pop purchased from
    K&G's.
        it fits great and only itches around my pant legs.
to jazz it up a bit, Star recommended I pair my suit
with a light gray dress shirt that has a white French collar,
and a navy, pink, and silver checkered tie.
I am complete with a pair of not-quite-midnight blue
square-toed Stacy Adams lace-up leather shoes with black taps at
    both ends.
        Pop said this will ensure the bottoms don't get too scuffed.

I feel like I look older than seventeen.
    I wish I was rocking an all-dark blue denim tuxedo,
    but Pop says a suit like this can also be worn to
        church,
    to work, to a job interview, to a funeral, to my
        graduation ceremony.

Ma looks happy and says to me, "you look so handsome, baby."
I look into the eyes of the first soul I ever saw
and smile back all the straight teeth she paid for from her empty
    pocketbook,
with no child-support payments from Pop.

suddenly, the house phone rings.
Ma picks up on the second chime and only one second after
hearing the voice on the other end, her entire face falls into itself.
she says, "you're going to have to tell him yourself."
and then she informs me that Pop has to tell me something about
    my limousine.

I grab the phone, "hey, Pop, what's wrong?"
"ay, Shorty Bus Stop, see, what had happened was . . ."
    he proceeds to tell me some story to explain why it's not his
        fault
    that me and Blu will not be riding to prom in a long, black
        luxury vehicle.
    and that to remedy the issue,
    he arranged for me to drive a rented beige four-door sedan,

complete with taupe fabric seats, power windows, and safety
    airbags.
he says he is on the way to bring this other car,
and praying I will not be too late picking up my date.

I can't apologize enough when I call Blu and inform her that I
    shall be arriving
in a 200-horse-powered pumpkin, instead of the 200-horse-drawn
    carriage.

although, no one seems to mind at all when I show up at her
    house,
dressed in my multipurpose evening wear, complete with a flower
    wrist corsage.

Mr. Anthony and Ms. Irene ask me to wait in the foyer of their
    big-ass home
because Blu is making her entrance from atop their staircase.
Blu's voice bounces down from heaven, "are y'all ready?"
Ms. Irene and I scream out in unison, "yes!"
Mr. Anthony responds, "Blu, stop all this nonsense and get your
    behind down here,
so that you and this boy can get out of my house and go to this
    party we paid for.
your mom and I have plans to make our own prom night in the
    living room tonight."

if they are like the Huxtables, then I'm definitely their son-in-law,

Elvin.

all of us have become a live audience laughing really hard at
ourselves.

"okay, here I come, cue the music."

then Blu's older brother Ronnie, who is standing in the nook right
off the grandiose steps,

presses the play button on his stereo boom box and it's

Lauryn Hill's version of "Can't Take My Eyes Off of You"
pumping out of the speakers.

Blu opens the bedroom door.

I hear the subtle sound of footsteps carefully walking on top of
carpet.

she is an angel gliding down the staircase in four-inch silver
strappy heels,

with shimmering stockings and a metallic gray ankle-length tube
dress.

her soft and fine black hair is twisted up toward the back in tiny
bantu knots

that leave just the right amount of follicles exposed to make tiny
fans.

she is wearing dark plum lipstick and I don't think anything else,

because nothing on her fresh face needs making up.

Blu is stunning and I am absolutely prepared for this moment
because without hesitation,

I suck in all the air surrounding my circumference

and I sing out at exactly the right time when Ms. Hill hits the chorus.

I say, "you look absolutely gorgeous, Blu."

her face becomes strawberry, and she responds,

"thanks, Tony, you're looking rather dapper yourself."

I start performing vanity by pretending to wipe fictional dust off
my shoulder tips

and smoothing out peach fuzz that is not growing on my invisible
goatee,

while licking my extra-moisturized lips like LL Cool J.

then, I place the corsage around her wrist.

we don't stop looking at each other while Ms. Irene takes our
pictures.

Mr. Anthony says to his wife, "that's enough, honey,

we need to get these hooligans out of here before I call the police

and report that there are some suspicious teenagers trespassing on
my property."

we walk to their driveway, and I open the passenger door for Blu.

then loop around the back of the car to enter on the driver's side,

and I see her reach over and press the unlock button,

which makes me smile because clearly, she is not a selfish person.

we both get buckled up in our seats,

and as I'm shifting the rental car's gear into reverse,

Blu places her hand over the top of mine and says,

"it's okay, Tony, we're going to have a blast tonight."

before we pull off, Mr. Anthony runs out of the house,

approaches my rented sedan, and asks me to roll my window down.
I follow suit and he looks right through me and Blu,
and says, "y'all better not make no babies tonight,
because we ain't taking care of nobody's grandkids."

Ms. Irene yells from behind him, "Anthony, leave them alone!"
Mr. Anthony echoes his wife, "uh huh, y'all better have some
    protection,"
and winks his eye at me as if he knows that I have one unexpired,
wrapped condom nestled in my front pocket next to my wallet,
neither of which I am sure that I will need to use tonight.

Blu and I both respond with some version of
"we won't, but if we decide to get busy, we're prepared,"
which seems to satisfy her stepfather's serious-ass joke.

we exit stage left, right before the playful interrogation
became an uncomfortable question-and-answer period about sex.

GETTING BUSY IS SERIOUS BUSINESS

Blu and I don't talk about what Mr. Anthony said during our car
    ride,
we just blast the radio, singing music, rapping songs, and talking
    about the world.
we don't discuss the script that we are naturally playing out either.
although, I know this is the evening we're supposed to get to
    fourth base,
I'm just gonna focus on having fun tonight,
because one thing about me and Blu is, we love a good party.

we pull up to DuVal High's senior prom,
step out of my sedan, and walk into a luxury-inspired event rental
    space
with a fancy French name, across the street from a PG strip mall.
this expensive-looking edifice is surrounded by my classmates
and their black luxury limousines, and their stretch Hummers,
and their tinted white Lincoln Navigators,
and their floor-length gowns, and their tuxedo striped pants.
there are extra-large mirrors, turquoise circular velvet furniture,
and gold-painted chandeliers lit up by tiny tea candle bulbs
hanging from the twenty-foot-high ceilings.

every single senior is a celebrity wearing our sunshades at sunset
and the paparazzi absolutely love us.

we head toward the check-in desk, where Bernice, our SGA
    president,
informs us that we are sitting at the same table with Bubba and
    Cubby,
both of whom are already inside with their dates.
she reminds me to cast my vote for the prom court competition
    and says,
"good luck, Tony Keith," with a smile suggesting there is
    something I should know.
and I am indeed surprised to see my name listed as one of the five
    nominees for prom king.
        the other four are a mixture of muscular athletes and
            handsome knuckleheads,
        all of whom are far more popular than me.
        so, I decide to fill in the bubble next to "Tony Keith" extra
            hard
        because at least one person would have voted for me.

then, I escort Blu inside the main room where the music is so thick
that girls are already transitioning from their shiny stilettos to
    matte ballet flats.
we: us both are instantly swept up in a vortex of seniors celebrating
    like it's 1999
before anybody could say 2000-00 party over,   oops, out of time.
we do not hesitate to make our way to the dance floor

where Juvenile, Lil Wayne, and Mannie Fresh are telling us to
    back our azzes up.
and 702 is asking the girls in the front and the back,
who were feeling that, to put one hand up,
while Donnell Jones sings, "U Know What's Up."
then, Jigga asks us over and over whether we knew his name,
and said that we better get it right.
and that's before the DJ starts playing the pocket on the song
    "Skillet" by Backyard Band,
followed up with Northeast Groovers' remix of the "Booty Call."

the crowd forms a circle around me and Blu as we dance close to
    each other,
smiling and laughing and sweating and singing loud and spinning
    around and dipping low.
we are happy together like this, loosely moving our bodies to the
    rhythm,
while everyone else and their dates are doing the exact same thing.

            as if music can erase borderlines between joy and freedom.

and it's only thirty minutes left to party, when the DJ announces
    that the time has come
to reveal the winners of this year's prom royal court.
Bubba, Cubby, and I have taken off our suit jackets
and loosened the knots from whatever fabric was formally tied
    around our necks
and we are using paper napkins to wipe the sweat off our faces.

Blu is sitting down with Candy; they are both fanning cool air
   into their warm faces.
I go and sit next to her and despite partying like a rock star, she
   has a completely flawless face.
the DJ tells us to simulate a drum roll and so, we bang on top of
   our tables,
and pat our hands up and down on our laps and stomp our feet on
   the ground quickly.

he continues with two-second pauses in between each word,
"and   the   winner   of
   DuVal High's   Class   of   1999
prom   queen   is   Tolu!"
everyone starts clapping their hands loudly and screaming for joy
as Tolu lifts the edge of her black lace gown making her way to the
   center,
where Ms. Peralta is waiting with a bejeweled tiara to place atop
   her hair.
my heart is now beating completely through my outermost layer of
   skin,
wondering who the person will be   instead of me,
to reign with Queen Tolu in the prom kingdom full of DuVal
   High seniors.

suddenly, my entire world stops moving.
I don't hear the drums rolling,
nor can I detect if the microphone is making an awkward
   squeal.

and I can barely see anything except a blurred picture of Bubba
     and Cubby
who are both standing in front of me holding unlit cigars in their
     mouths,
and two bottles of apple cider in each hand.
they are saying, "congrats, Tone Capone!" over and over.
I shake my head left to right a few times and say, "wait, what?"
then I hear the DJ go, "y'all, let's give another round of applause
for your prom king, Tony Keith."
everything comes back into focus,
and I recognize that I am indeed alive
and that I did not press pause on real life because it hurts when I
     pinch myself.
I am not dreaming.

I run one hundred miles a second to meet Queen Tolu and we hug
     hard.
then Ms. Peralta gives me a full embrace and says, "felicidades, el
     rey Keith"
while placing a black and silver satin crown on my puck full of
     knowledge.

I jump up without falling over my not-so-midnight blue shoes,
and with right fist pumped toward the sky, I scream out, "woooo
     hoooo!"
then, I look over at Blu, who is smiling from ear to ear,
obviously proud of her regal boyfriend,
and I wonder if she, too, is thinking about the next thing
that the script is telling us that we are supposed to do.

BASEMENTS ARE DARK FOR A REASON

I drove Blu back to her house.
she uses the garage entrance to get in the house most of the time
because, like me, she often loses her front-door keys.
she gave me the combination a while ago,
she tells me to come back in five minutes,
just so she could confirm her parents were asleep: they are.

we are on the lower level of their single-family home,
with all its plush carpet and comfy furniture.
the only light is coming from the floor-model television
playing a Billy Blanks Tae Bo infomercial.
we are pretending to watch this muscular Black man
sell VHS tapes of himself performing martial arts fitness,
while kissing each other hard on the mouth.

Blu and I quickly round second base, which ain't unfamiliar
    territory for us.
and after some awkward trial and error,
and a little trembling with thunder, we steal our way to third base.
but we ain't got long to stay here, because the trumpets are
    sounding,

which is a signal that the trees are bending.

so, we approach the plate, with our eyes set on making the final
    play
by gently sliding into fourth base.
I have unwrapped the glove that was stored inside my pants
    pocket,
which is no longer situated around my lower limbs.
        I made sure to pinch it at the tip when I put it on
        to ensure there is enough space
        for my energy to escape when the time comes.
                                    my stomach hurts.
                            and while I cannot see It,
                I hear the Boogeyman whispering in my head.
            It is telling me that the main objective of this game
                        of getting busy baseball
                        is to win the most points,
            which can only occur after several rounds of catch, pitch,
                                        and kiss,
and then running around until one of us brings the most batters in
                            before our time runs out
                    or one of us   strikes out.
and I can't figure out why this feels like
I am playing the right game, but on the wrong field.
I do not think my equipment is designed to complement Blu's
    team,
let alone push my way through them with enough force to hit a
    home run.

we launch the first ball and I stretch my arm out and up
hoping that whatever we hit in the air will land firmly in my palm.
but the Boogeyman reminds me that I've got these butterfingers,
and so, what we sent out in space has already slipped through my
    soft hands,
causing the glove to keep falling off.
I am unable to levitate above the outfield.

                        It keeps asking me if I remember Darin's scent,
                                    if I am aware I am a sissy,
                    if I understand straight boys don't ask these questions,
                            if I am preparing my soul to burn for eternity.
I am not hot.
        I am not flaming.
                nor am I on fire.
and it is not long before Blu and I both decide
that our game of getting busy baseball should be considered a tie,
despite being only a few feet away from reaching home plate.

I don't know if Blu is as disappointed with me
as I am about myself right now,
but her spirit is calm, and her energy is warm enough
to break through the icy tension that I feel rising up from my
    ankles.

we put our clothes back on,
resettle the cushions on the sofa,
and clear up any evidence that would prove we flexed our

Get Out of Hell Free hall passes on prom night.

while sitting with our legs crossed over one another, Blu asks,
"what do you think college will be like for us?
do you see us still being together?"

I say, "honestly, I love you, Blu, and I can't imagine being with
    anyone else.
I also can't predict the future, but somehow, I know that you and I
    are always
going to be a significant part of each other's lives,
regardless of if we go to the same college, or get married to each
    other,
or make beautiful babies together."

Blu snuggles herself into my right armpit and says,
"yeah, I feel the same exact way, I love you too."

we skipped the script after leaving Blu's prom.
instead of playing games of getting busy baseball in her basement,
we watched reruns of *Martin* and ate buttered popcorn mixed with
    fruit snacks.

IT WON'T LET ME SLEEP

my covers aren't heavy enough to hold me as tight as I need them
    to
and ain't nothing but dust collecting on my pillow every time I
    blink,
thinking about how much I want to be with Blu,
but not in the getting busy way,
not in the let's pay for an expensive wedding and have kids way.

I want all the fairy tale and fantasy of love
but without all the Boogeyman's bullshit.

and all that praying to Jesus is teaching me
that there is some form of freedom found in my poems.
    somehow, those metaphors wrap themselves around my skin,
making it easier for me to walk through the world in camouflage
pretending my girl-friends are girlfriends.
I can hide, become invisible, and disappear in them.

I arm myself with everything I got,
and it takes two poems to write the Boogeyman away   for now.

UNTITLED

constant smiles wear my face
mixed emotions keep my heart paced
undying thoughts of those undying memories
feeling immortal, living on for centuries
butterflies fly rings inside
feelings of hate and guilt have off and died
to be loved gives you great feelings
kills all bad emotions and brings about believing
to be loved is to answer questions not yet asked
feeling the future and remembering the past
not forgetting that beautiful face
passing through my head at an untimely pace
needing the attention and greedy for affection
to be loved is a feeling far expressed
to be loved would be to hate less.

Constant smiles wear my face
~~Con~~ Mixed emotions keep my heart paced
Undying thoughts of those undying memories
Feeling immortal, living on for centuries
~~For the love of so much beauty~~
Butterflies fly rings ~~confinedly~~ inside
Feelings of hate and guilt have offed and died.
To be loved gives you great feelings
Kills all bad emotions and brings out the loving.
To be loved answering questions not yet asked
Feeling the future and remembering the past
Not forgetting that ~~one~~ beautiful face
passing through my head ~~constantly~~ at an untimely pace
Needing the attention and ~~keep~~ greeding the affection
To be loved a feeling far expressed
To be loved would be ~~too~~ to hate less.

UNTITLED

I feel like screaming to the top of my lungs
Make my brain malfunction until the next day's begun
I want to run outside and scream out all the pain
and when the dark clouds run by they wash it with the rain
I want to yell and shout until midnight when the moon is still
I want to call out your name in my worst nightmare
I want to just burst out in tears whenever you're there
I wanna scream from the pit of my stomach
to the end of my tongue
I wanna love you like I never loved anyone.

I feel like screaming to the top of my
lungs
Make my brain malfunction until
the nexts days begun
I want to run outside and scream out
all the pain
And when the dark clouds run by
They wash it with the rain
I want to yell and shout until
midnight when the moon is still
I want to call out your name in my
worst nightmare
I want to just burst out in tears
whenever your there
I wanna scream from the pit of my
stomach to the end of my tounge
I wanna love you
I never loved anyone.

RISE AND SHINE

I dreamt that I was at a basement party standing in front of a
    microphone,
wearing a superhero cape made of metaphors,
and my eyes were shut tight as I focused on every single breath of
    some poem
because I wanted to make sure that my lungs had the capacity
to create words that defied the laws of gravity,
and that swirled into a vortex of knowledge
that caused all these supernatural catastrophes.
I don't remember where the event took place,
nor do I recall any faces from the audience,
but having poetry come to the rescue makes a lot of sense to me.

it smells as if Ma is casting a cooking spell and she must be in a
    real good mood
because she is also playing music on her record player.
I jump out of bed, put on sweatpants and a T-shirt, wash my face,
    and brush my teeth
while singing and dancing to "Cat in the Hat" by Little Benny &
    the Masters,
"Sardines" by Junk Yard Band, "Run Joe" by Chuck Brown,

"Joy and Pain" by Rob Base & DJ E-Z Rock, "The Show" by
    Doug E. Fresh & Slick Rick.

I enter the dining room and see Ma and Tamu are seated at the
    table
with their plates full of warm home cooking stacked up high in
    front of them.
"we're out of bacon," Ma says, giving me a smile and digging a
    fork into her breakfast.
"dang, for real?" I say.
"that boy loves him some bacon," Tamu says, causing me to crack
    my first smile of the day.
Ma says, "go make yourself a plate, and there's an envelope
    addressed to you from MSU.
I left it for you on the kitchen counter."

I blink. I catch. I stop breathing.

I snatch the eight-and-a-half by eleven-inch stuffed container
full of important papers about my post-secondary fate and it says,

"Dear Anthony R. Keith, Jr.,
Congratulations on your acceptance . . .
. . . However, SAT scores . . . Math: 500 . . . English: 460 . . .
. . . might need remediation . . . placement test required to declare
    business major . . .
. . . school year 1999–2000 tuition and fees: $7,535
. . . FAFSA determined eligible for loans . . . subsidized:

$3,000 . . . unsubsidized: $5,500 . . .

. . . However, no grants awarded . . . total aid: $8,500 . . .

. . . mandatory first-year student orientation . . . enrollment
deposit due: $100 . . ."

I wasn't expecting MSU's acceptance letter to come by and bop me
    upside the head
all hard like this,
        smashed the Boogeyman's face in a bit
            shook It off Its axis.
I take a deep sigh, relieved I am no longer scared about getting
    into college.

I drop my arms around Ma's neck while she is sitting down,
and she grabs ahold of me with her soft and unwrinkled hands.
we both squeeze each other tight and she says, "I'm so proud of
    you, baby, I mean it.
you really *can* do anything, can't you?"

                                                    I don't have an answer.
"but, I can't afford to pay that tuition," she says.
"Ma, I know, look, I've already done the math in my head,
if I accept the full amount of loans, I will have about $1,000 of aid
    left
to cover any additional charges.
plus, I've been saving money from my Old Navy paychecks every
    two weeks,
and I can use that for books or whatever."

"baby, how are you going to pay all that money back after you
    graduate?"
I know that I don't have any power over whatever will happen in
    the future,
so, I tell Ma that per usual, when the time comes: I'll figure it out.

I get my grub on but don't pig out on Ma's best breakfast plate
before I call everyone and give them the great news!

Cubby goes, "let's go, Tone Lōc!, I'll see you there!"
Bubba goes, "congrats, Tone Capone, I got into Temple!"
Tiffy goes, "so proud of you, sweetie, I'll be at UMD!"
Ebby goes, "told you so, brother, we'll be neighbors!"
Aunt Tee goes, "alright, nephew, that's what I'm talking about!"
Pop goes, "eyes haven't seen . . ."
Tolu goes, "I knew it! I knew it! I knew it!"
Blu goes, "looks like we'll be there together, Tony!"
        the Boogeyman goes, "oh yes, I'm coming with you."

I GUESS WE'LL GO TOGETHER

I am a goldfish inside of a crystal-clear glass bowl,
infinitely swimming around in circles with the other Class of 1999
    graduates.
and we are all being watched by every single person in the world
as we walk in procession, organized according to our last names,
so that everyone in our family knows the order in which their kid
    will officially
walk across the stage and enter adulthood   for real for real.

all our cheerleaders are staring down into the center of the arena
from up top in the balcony bleachers,
where they are unafraid to blast their airhorns
and hold up their homemade poster boards
and screen-printed T-shirts with our baby pictures.
I am seated too many rows up and way more than two seats over
    from Bubba and Cubby,
so, I have to keep looking over my shoulder to look at them
and laugh at everything there is for us to find funny about this
    moment.

I show Cubby that I'm wearing my blue and white Jason Kidds
instead of my not-so-midnight blue square-toed Stacy Adams.

213

he mouths the word "jeepers," which makes me ball over in
    heartful silent chuckle.
I'm trying to avoid snorting, while thinking of when we met in
    fifth grade,
and I was wearing a pair of Sears brand sneakers on my first day,
with grass stain patches on my hand-me-down baggy jeans.
                            it hurt then, but for some reason, not now.

it is hot as hell and my skin is itching underneath my suit
that I layered underneath my graduation gown.
all this polyester smothering all the lotion I rubbed on this morning.
there is a pool of sweat falling from my forehead,
causing the square cap and its dangling tassel to keep sliding
    toward the back
        where the puck used to be,
and so, I have to keep pushing it back in place.

Tolu is delivering the valedictorian speech,
and says that there comes a time in life when one must reflect
and thank those who have played an impacting role in our lives.
she says how grateful she is to God, her family, teachers, and
    friends,
because without them, she would not exist.
I feel like she is looking directly at me too
when she expresses special gratitude to her "shining stars,"
because they were reliable enough
to stick with her when things got tough.

whole time, I can't imagine what Tolu's life was like
outside of the time we spent together at DuVal High,
but somehow, I think I understand exactly what she means.
however, my weighted anchor has always been the Boogeyman's
      voice
and Its reflection in the mirror.
but I am learning that the more I hear my own voice
speaking through my words on pages,
and in the poems that I perform on stages,
the more clearly my body is reflecting freedom.
        I am starting to look like love, which is like kryptonite to the
            Boogeyman.
        love is Its Achilles' heel.
        love is Its mushy part.
        love is Its soft spot.
        love is Its vulnerable core.
        love is Its exposed center.
        love is exposing Its internalized phobias.

and It is deathly afraid of knowing that light cannot avoid
sticking to the brown on my Black skin.
plus, I am going to an HBCU, so, for sure, at MSU,
I'll learn to love me   and all people like me more.
which means, I'll have no choice but to become a goofy
      romantic scholar.

                              the Boogeyman is like,
"so, are you bound to get married and make babies with Blu?"

I ignore Its voice and focus as Tolu's closing her speech,
"my success is dedicated to all those who doubted me, tried to
    hinder my success,
and especially those who 'hated' on my skills, look at me now!"
her voice is vibrating a victorious energy
and I am crying warm and slow tears,
thinking about how much I am going to miss watching her take
    tedious notes
and listening to her wisdom face-to-face five days a week.

Principal Burns follows Tolu's speech with a bag full of vague
    words about
four years feeling like an eternity,
and about us beginning a new journey beyond DuVal High's
    hallways.
he says that we will face a multitude of challenges,
        without explaining why this is the case,
            nor why he knows it to be some truth about the future of
                Black kids.
then he reminds us that every experience offers its own rewards
    and lessons learned.

                I think he makes a great point because despite all the chaos
                                    erupting around me
                        since the night of my parents' squabble,
                    I figured out a way to get myself into college.
    that's gotta mean something   about me   right?

FALL 1999

THIS IS NOT EVEN FUNNY.

I live in O'Connell Hall (OC), an all-boys residence on south
    campus,
the opposite side of MSU where Blu stays in Blount Towers
and where Cubby lives in Rawlings Hall.
truth is, I hate it here, and I know that's a strong word,
but this space has been nothing but a hamster wheel of misfortune
    and torture.

first of all, it stinks.
there are no air-conditioning units so the late September heat
is screaming all its glory on top of and down through Herring Run
    Park,
        a tributary of Baltimore's Back River flowing directly in the
            back of OC.
this building smells like whatever wildlife is swimming inside *that*
    water,
specifically went there to die because it knows that there is no
    other outlet
for its flesh to decompose with any real dignity,
other than the local piping hot sewage behind a building of
    collegiate Black boys.

Star cleaned my room when she and Pop dropped me off,
so the aroma in here is more like a bouquet of bleach and fresh
    flowers
and a slimy garbage dumpster full of wet trash
are fighting for air supremacy,
but none of them can win,
so they just huff and puff on pieces of shit
while spitting the leftover feces directly into each other's faces.
and that's exactly what this space is:
        a receptacle for odors to exist as ghosts that fly in and out of
            OC's cement walls,
        complete with sandstone linoleum floors, wooden beds on
            platforms
        with six-inch navy blue sleeping pads pretending to be plush
            twin mattresses.

second of all, I'm still adjusting to living with my roommate
    Boots.
he arrived a few days after me,
pulled up in a white Crown Victoria with tinted windows,
two hubcaps with paper-thin treads on three of his tires,
and a dent in the fender that barely lets his license plate dangle
    horizontally.

he came carrying two duffle bags packed full of unfolded lumps of
    clothes   that's it.

Boots has smooth almond skin, a bleached white straight smile,

a yellow-orange ring around his brown eyes,
and short dried-out twists that are always partially covered
by a navy blue beanie rolled up around the edges.

most days my roommate walks around barefoot inside of his gray
    fuzzy slippers,
or he'll wear white tube socks with black flattened open-toe
    athletic slides.

we are about the same height, but Boots carries his weight in his
    chest,
        the only area on his body that he wants to build up to appear
        bigger than his scrawny stick-figure legs can stand on.
we get along well, but don't spend much time together outside of
    our room.
                        and I'm absolutely okay with that.
he knows that Blu and I go together,
but not that I think that I'm gay,
                  and I plan to keep it that way.

third of all, I can't think "straight."
it's hard pretending that living amongst all these Black boys is an
    easy feat
while my imagination is running wild half the time.
when we arrived, I was shocked to see so many of them: us: we
    busy
lifting heavy bags and carrying bulky boxes across our thresholds
    of young manhood.

we were all sweating a little heavy,
and those of us that were still wearing shirts
were using the bottom hem to wipe the salty water
oozing from out of our shiny foreheads and in between our
    mahogany clavicles,
        briefly exposing our stomachs and happy trails and boxer
            short brands
        and bellty buttons and belt buckles and flies unzipped.

a few of my fellow OC mates were looking directly into my eyes
as we all wandered around the hallways meeting and greeting folks
                living on different floors of our stacked residence.
some of them stared at me a little longer than some of the others,
                        and I wondered if Kyle was right
                when he told me in the chat room that at some point,
a moment will come when I'll have the answer to my question.

I DON'T TELL ANY OF THIS TO ANYONE

especially not Blu, who I'm meeting at the Refac for dinner
   tonight.
she's still pissed at me for not calling her when I arrived on the
   first day.
      it's just that it took me a while to figure out how the phones
         work on campus,
      and by the time I finally dialed the right extension, she didn't
         pick up.
      I didn't know how to navigate campus at night, so I wound
         up in my room   alone,
      eating care-package snacks for dinner.

      Blu says she waited hours for her line to ring that evening
      before leaving with her roommate Dayanna to get food.
      says I "ghosted her."

for real for real, I think she's been disappointed with me since
   prom night,
but neither of us are saying anything about it   out loud.
      it's as if we both know that what didn't go down in the
         basement

probably wouldn't be going down in our college dorms either,
where visitation *between* boys and girls is a privilege,
     but ain't no policies about boys and girls being *with*
each other . . .

Cubby is gonna join us too, I haven't seen him since summer
     orientation
          when my advisor set me up for 8 a.m. classes three days a
               week.
          when my financial aid barely paid the bill, but got me some
               books.
          when I tested college-ready for English Comp I, despite what
               the SAT said.
          when I couldn't tour OC because it was closed for asbestos.

Boots and I are walking to the Refac together.
"c'mon, Tony!" he says, trying to convince me for the umpteenth
     time
to lift weights in the gym with him and a few of his friends.

"Boots, I already told you, I ain't interested in bulking up nothing
but the neurons inside of my brain
by lifting books to my face and lowering them down very slowly,"
     I respond.

"you're such a nerd, roommate."

                                   I'm okay with this too.

he laughs, followed by a heavy cough caused by all the cigarettes
    he smokes.
"I'm telling you, Tony, I could teach you how to *at least* bench-
    press
one hundred percent of your total body weight.
that way if you're being attacked,
you can be strong enough to tackle your perpetrator."
        which is always what he says, while performing a marathon
            of push-ups
        on *our* dusty linoleum floor next to the dumbbell he curls up
            and down
        while rocking back and forth on his chalky feet.
                    I can't be too sure, but I don't think that he be
                        practicing good form.

I say, "nope, not interested" and shake my head.
he goes, "alright, but one of these days, I'm gonna get you to go
    with me,
and then you'll begin to love feeling the burn."
then he tightens his face and lifts both biceps up to his ears,
as if his posturing will convince me otherwise.
"yeah, we'll see, Boots, just keep on trying, my brotha,"
I say, offering him empty hope.

we make our way past the Verda Freeman Welcome Bridge
and I spot a flyer taped to one of the light poles that says:
"Poetry Slam 2Morrow Nite, 7 pm, McKeldin Center, first prize:
    $25"

I'm a broke poet, whose family ain't sent me a dollar, nickel, or dime,
and so $25 would be like hitting the lottery.
Boots is carrying on and on while I'm wondering about the poems:
    the ones that become the winners,
        and about the poets who be writing them
           and if they're fighting their own Boogeypeople.

Boots don't know about my poems.
I packed up the box from underneath my bed
and stashed it in a chest that Ma put in the attic of her new house.
I wouldn't want him to discover my poetic secrets.
    too scared to write in pen and on paper
     without having a private space to store my hoard,
       so I've been keeping everything inside of my head.

truth is, I haven't written any poems since I've been here,
words ain't launching from beyond the stars like they used to.
as if something is blocking them from breaking through their
    solar barriers.

I never feel like I am on fire whenever I am around my roommate
    either,
                  and I'm also absolutely okay with that too.
Boots and I approach the back of Rawlings Hall and there is a
    small crowd of students
standing in front of a six-foot table with a tall banner that says
    "FREE."
I tell him that I'll meet him inside the Refac and go see what all

the buzz is about.

there are representatives from College Student Visa
and they are giving away logo T-shirts, pens, water bottles, and
　　squishy-squeezy stress balls.
I ease my way up to overhear a short round Black man saying that
　　if I got a job, then I am eligible to apply for their credit card
with a guaranteed limit of $500 and a 0% APR for the first three
　　months.

　　　　　　　　　　I don't know what the hell any of this means,
　　　　　　　　　　but $500 is one hundred times more than
　　　　　　　　what I can withdraw from the ATM right now.
　　　　　　　　　plus, I am a seasonal employee at Old Navy
　　　　　　　　and the holidays are the busiest time of the year,
　　　　　　　　　　　　so technically I'm working.
　　　　　　　it's not like I can't afford to *not* do this, right?

I complete the free application that came with all these free gifts
and I fall in a single-file line to get inside of the Refac.

THE CAMPUS IS ALIVE HERE

one thing about MSU is, everyone is fresh dressed like a million
     bucks   but me.
I've no idea how they can afford to own such fashionable
     wardrobes,
and all I got are Old Navy high school clothes that got me looking
     like a juvenile
in the presence of Black women wearing leather tube tops and
     cropped T-shirts,
gold hoop earrings, paisley printed skirts, boxed braids, bandanas,
stepping boots, bucket caps, and thick sunshades,
the fellas be in Timberlands, oversized white tees, puffer jackets,
denim overalls, Starter jackets, luxury tracksuits, camouflage
     shirts, and fitted caps.
                              and they'll be dressed like this by noon,
               while I've been in class for four hours adorned in basics.

most students be in the Refac grouped up by some algorithm
that determines your place in the ocean of MSU's collegiate
     scholars,
simply based on your answer to the question, "where are you
     from?"

which for me is always a long-ass story,
and so I don't feel like I fit in anywhere.

it smells like freshly deep-fried donuts covered in powdered sugar,
garlic powder, table salt, and ground black pepper in here.
for dinner, I always eat fried chicken tenders and thick-cut oily
    french fries
with the salty soupy yellow cheese sauce.
unless it's steak teriyaki stir-fry night, when the white rice be a
    little crunchy
but the beef is always seasoned just right.

I don't spot Boots anywhere in here   he wanders,
but I see Blu and Dayanna with their trays,
walking to grab a seat at a table that Cubby already secured for us.

"Tōne-loc!" Cubby shouts out.
"what's up, dawg!" I yell back.
"hey Dayanna!"
"hey Tony Tone!" she says, while hopping in the chair next to
    Cubby,
laying her pressed straight long black hair across her left shoulder.
    They're clearly crushing on each other
    and I wonder if she might be my boy-friend's very first
        girlfriend.

    Rawlings Hall and Blount Towers are right next to each
        other

and Blu says Cubby is always in their room,
or that she be chilling in his quad while his suitemates are
out.
Blu turns around and smiles behind her eyes and through her
teeth
without parting her pink puffy lips
and we hug without pressing into each other too hard or for too
long.
"hey babe," we say in unison.

Cubby joined MSU's marching band as a saxophonist
and is telling us how excited he is about playing in the
homecoming parade,
while Dayanna is looking at him all googly-eyed.
                                    The script was made for them.
Boots walks over to us with two unpeeled oranges in his hand
and a Ziploc bag full of dried cornflakes with sugar layered on the
bottom.
we don't ask any questions.
He goes, "what's up, everybody? Hey roommate!"
    as if I am not a part of the general collective.
Then he leans over and whispers in my ear,
"I'm gonna go see Chuck Brown at the 9:30 club tonight,
can I borrow the green sweater your grandma gave you for
Christmas?"
                        he be all up in my business and deep in my closet,
                                    which I don't mind,
            'cause I know what it's like to wear clothes that don't belong

to you first.

"sure Boots, just don't smoke while you're wearing it."

as if he can help it.

then,   he   has   the   nerve   to   say   OUT LOUD,
"Blu, I told Tony to put a sock on the door if y'all want some
     privacy tonight, alright?"
and then he winks at us before exiting stage left,
right before Dayanna says, "I invited Cubby over to help me study,
so if y'all wanted to chill at OC until visiting hours are up, that'd
     be cool."

I can't tell if she is asking permission, expecting input,
                          or making a decision
                     about our split couples night.

Blu and I do need time to talk in person about things without any
     interruption,
so I say, "I think that's a great idea."
she responds, "I think so too."

231

IT'S ICE COLD IN HERE.

we're supposed to be sizzling hot.

we're supposed to be falling all over each other by now.

we're supposed to desire to be closer than our outer flesh is
rubbing right now.

we're supposed to feel warmth when we kiss.

we're supposed to fit on this twin bed together although it's too
small for us both.

we're supposed to want to be all tangled up in a web of ourselves,
right?

we're supposed to be tearing our clothes off uncontrollably like
they do in the movies.

Blu says, "stop."

I say, "okay."

Blu says, "you've been distant."

I tell her, "you ain't lying."

Blu asks, "why are you so far away?"

I tell her, "I don't know."

Blu asks, "is it me?"

I tell her, "it's not you."

Blu asks, "if it's not me, then what is it?"

the Boogeyman says, "I know why."
I tell her, "I'm fine, just got a lot on my mind."
Blu asks, "like what?"
I tell her, "like stuff."
Blu says, "okay fine."
I say, "okay fine."

I wonder what Blu's tears taste like,
whether they're warm and salty like mine.
if we're both sad or relieved
or something in between
love and mourning.

we say, maybe we both need space.
we say, we've always been friends at the core.
we say, breaking up won't change who we are.
we say, we'll see each other all the time.
we say, we'll call every day anyway.
we say, we'll plan a study day next week.
we say, we'll let people figure out that it's over.
we say, we're good.
we mean all of this.
and we do not kiss
when I take the sock off the door
and walk with Blu down the hall
and to the front desk to collect her ID
and request that she call me as soon as she gets to her room.

MY PHONE DOESN'T RING.

I decide that perhaps it is best to make use of the community
   shower
before the bulk of the other Black boys living on this floor
return for the remainder of the evening.

the room is empty, save for the sounds of people
laughing from outside of a caged window carved out somewhere
   near the ceiling.
I flip the light switch on the wall up and down a few times to
   confirm
that after a few seconds of blinking,
the ceiling lamp bulbs are indeed doing the absolute best they can,
and that this barely visible sunset is as bright as it's going to get in
   here.

I navigate to the last stall on the end because for some reason
being farther away from the main door feels less scary.

I am petrified with fear the moment I lower my head
and allow the lukewarm water
to rinse the bar soap suds off my neck, back, and shoulders.

because someone enters the room, turns off the ceiling lights,
and doesn't say a word.
it is too dark to feel safe, so I hold my breath and keep quiet,
    as if there are no sounds emitting from my stall,
        including my failed theatrical attempt to perform as a
            silently dead person,
    who is also taking a shower.

I don't see anyone's shadow, but I call out to their energy.
"hello, there's someone in here!" I yell out in a harmless tone,
assuming that perhaps they do indeed believe that I am not alive,
    and that I am also trying to clean myself.
there is no response.
"hello!" I repeat.

then, I hear a faint sound of footsteps shuffling toward the
    direction
where my ankles and flip-flops are visible beneath the shower
    curtain.

SLAM!

I hear the main door shut fast and tight.
"ah!" I scream and peek from behind the curtain.
whoever was just a few feet away has now run out at the speed of
    light,
which they failed to turn back on once they left.

I am partially painted in suds and soaked wet   120 lbs.,
with my towel draped loosely around me,

when I grab my shower caddy and balled-up boxer shorts,
while darting to my room, still inhaling all my breath.

I am surprised to discover that there is no one in the hallway
waiting to laugh at some prank they pulled.
no person is there chuckling and pointing at my dripping body
as I fumble through the door to my room,
while peering over my right shoulder and turning the lock
   clockwise.

                              what just happened?
                              did I make it all up?
                              was it the Boogeyman?
                           why wasn't It chasing me then?
I drop all my things, sans towel, on the linoleum floor,
and lay my right hand over my chest,
feeling how hard my heart is working to keep me alive.
then I look up at the mirror
that's probably been mounted on the wall next to my wooden
   platform bed
ever since the OC was built.

I stare at myself covered in cold water,
looking both scared and scary.

I blink enough times to realize that I have once again become the
   Boogeyman in the mirror
                  I need to find a way to protect my peace inside of OC.

I slide the towel across my soapy skin, removing layers of the
remaining ivory foam
and water droplets sliding through my goose bumps until I am
dry.
I put on a pair of navy blue basketball shorts,
and an overworn fire red Old Navy logo T-shirt
and bury myself beneath my new comforter.
inhale:
boiled eggs, vanilla ice cream, blue crab guts, maraschino cherries,
morning breath, maple syrup, melting rubber, overripe bananas
exhale.

I close my eyes and just let the tears fall into puddles,
praying to God that He won't let me drown.

I AIN'T SAFE HERE.

it's 2:44 a.m.

I've got bags full of sleeping sand sagging underneath my lower
    eyelids.
the sheer weight of them have pulled my entire vision down,
exposing the pink and puffy tissue, blue veins, and red blood
    vessels
and layers of skin that should be protecting my sand-paper-bag
    eyes
from flying debris.

I look at Boots's bed and see the plastic cover on his mattress pad
    is peeling off
right in the back corner where his slobber collects at night.
I wonder about his hygiene.

then, I shift my weary gaze to the monitor of my all-in-one
    personal computer
which, like Star asked, Pop put on top of the counter.

with no safe place in this shared space

to hide my handwritten poetry incantations,
I decided it was time to battle the Boogeyman with a poem typed
   up on the screen.

like several of my poems, the subject of this one shows up as a
   feminine image,
but this piece ain't got nary a thing to do with Blu
and absolutely everything to do with me.
     so, it's personal,
        and so, perhaps, poetically,
            it's just an expression of personification.

INFINITY

I'm in love with something called "Infinity"
she is exceptional in her beauty
and majestic in her divinity
she told me that she would last forever
and that time was of no essence
and that everything inside me would remain
as long as I remain humble in her presence

Infinity had everything
that a desperate man would desire
she had the face of an angel
the breath of a cloud
and passion like a fire
she knew how to touch me
and cause immortal pleasure
she promised me eternal happiness
and a predestined treasure

Infinity said that first,
I must admit my love
and that the witness to this statement

sits on clouds above
she said I must make an oath
to her and be honest
and a marriage to my soul
would be her infinite promise

and as I began to secrete those words
from my lips
I got a numbness in my toes,
my pelvis, and my fingertips
and I became surprised
the moment I realized
Infinity was no longer before my eyes
she'd become a cloud in the sky

and when I looked to my left
there was a mirror, with I in reflection
and what Infinity said
began to make a connection

so, I turned to the mirror, and I said,
"I'm in love with something called Infinity
and in that, as king I'll throne
eternity is my life's wishes
and my destiny, I own."

POETS ARE EVERYWHERE

I needed to breathe some kind of air that wasn't emanating from
    OC's walls
and decided to check out the poetry slam at the McKeldin Center
    tonight.
all the people with poems powerful enough to win prizes are
    sequestered together
although no one here knows my name or that I came here alone.
      everyone else got hype people giving them all this gas,
        fueling up their tank, revving up their engines for the major
          race,
        and I'm wheeling myself around on fumes and hope.

the host, Joseph, is a six-foot-two brown man
with a boulder holding down the bass in his voice,
and tattoo sleeves that look like robotic arms.
he is a member of the campus activities board
and asks if there are any more folks who want to compete tonight.
whole time, all I got is a folded piece of paper with my poem
    "Infinity" on it
      I've been saying over and over in my head,
        and it still don't make sense, but I'm familiar with the flow.

I don't know anything about battling poetry,
I just came to watch it all go down,
but I do know I need $25, so I sign myself up.

I am clearly unprepared when Joseph introduces the judges,
who were randomly selected from the audience of MSU students,
and lays out the rules for the slam:
three rounds

    first poem is three minutes.

    second poem is two minutes.

    third poem is one minute.

    no props for your poems.

I'm used to my stomach hurting, but tonight it's extra sensitive.
I feel like there's something boiling in my belly
that wants to exit my body in its warm liquid form.
I can't sit comfortably, and my private parts have seized up and
    shrank down
to withhold whatever energy left I'mma need to expel to get
    through this moment.

Joseph must've smelled how fresh and unqualified I was,
and so he called me up as the "sacrificial poet,"
    the one willing to pay the costs of life for my poems
      so that the judges have a benchmark to score the *real*
      competition.
I got one whole poem in my pocket that takes me twenty-nine
    seconds to read

only three people clap when I'm done sharing my secrets
to an audience who couldn't relate to the metaphors
  the cryptic messages I'm writing to keep the Boogeyman
   away.

the judges don't give any feedback,
they just hold their scores up on pieces of paper
from lowest to highest: 6, 6.5, 6.7
my scores totaled 19.2 out of 30 and Joseph thanks me for my
  participation.

I don't remain at the slam to watch who wins,
I walk to the OC thinking how being onstage when the audience
  are strangers,
   unfamiliar faces who show up to be moved on purpose,
was not something I was ready for.

but I know now, poetry hits people different if the poems they
  share
are solely meant to serve their own selfish purposes.
and ain't nothing wrong with that,
but I don't wanna compete with my poems.

I just want the audience to identify with the words
and to be able to perform my poetry in a way that is free
and relatable to at least one person in the audience.
  some human being needing a reminder of their humanity.

IT'S TOUGH BEING FIRST TO LOSE A BATTLE.

I'm almost to my room when I notice a sky-high giant walking
    toward me
with the campus ID he just collected from the front desk
after escorting some young woman   whose face I couldn't see
out into the darkness that lives beyond the OC.

"hey, that's your room, right?" he says, while pointing directly at
    my door
and smiling a set of bright headlights that are fastened to the front
of a Mack Truck that is his mouth.
"yeah," I respond, as we meet somewhere in the middle
and stand close enough to smell each other.

            I am trying to avoid acknowledging the obvious reality
                    that this moving statue is not wearing a shirt,
        not unless he considers his thick chest and folded hairy belly
                is a reasonable layer for covering absolutely nothing up.

"oh yeah, I thought so," he says.
        and based on the way his sweat shorts are situated dead center,
                    he is also not wearing anything underneath
            to conceal the crystal-clear evidence that he is still settling

himself down
from getting busy with that young woman.

I am controlling my unspoken curiosity
about what another Black man's nude body actually looks like
in real life,
especially when he is aroused,
and wondering how my body would feel
if I were to press my naked self against one.

he tells me that his name is Calvin,
and that was his girlfriend who had just stopped by, but she goes
to Coppin State.

"I think I saw a very pretty girl leaving your room the other night
too, playa,"
he says, while squinting his eyes together,
raising his right eyebrow above its equator,
and sticking his bright pink tongue out to the left side of his
mouth.

I don't say anything about my and Blu's amicable break-up besides,
"oh yeah, that *was* my girl, but you know how things go in college,
right?"
as if covertly inquiring about whether we are both reading the
same book
that for real for real only makes sense to one of us,
and that person ain't me.

Calvin responds, "bruh, who are you telling?
it's so much punany to get up here and all the girls got phat
    booties!"
he signals me to join him in a high five,
I guess to confirm some delusion he has about his irresistible
    power
over women's ability to resist having sex with him.

I am performing as straight as possible, and so, I meet his right
    palm
midway in the air with my right hand,
and our skin connects for a brief second of platonic bonding
before I change the subject.

I ask, "did you see anything to eat or drink in the vending
    machines?"
"nah man, there ain't shit in there
and I was just talking to our resident director about that yesterday.
he just keeps saying that it's coming soon."

I take a deep sigh and blow air out of my lips hard,
so that they flap open and closed, causing my face to sound like a
    propeller jet.
"that's exactly what he told me too, Calvin," I say.
"I'm not sure he knows what he's talking about."
he nods in agreement and begins our descent,
"alright, I'm about to go grab a shower, T."

                                    he gave me a nickname.

"are you gonna be around this weekend?" he asks.
"I'm not sure, I may go home,
all depends on what my bank account is looking like."

                                        I am telling the truth.
"word, I'll be around, that's my room right there."
he points down the hall and two doors down and across the way
from the staircase with the broken fire extinguisher.

"cool, I'll see you around."
then, I exit stage right, burning up, flaming, parched and starving,
smelling all that Calvin has left for me to consume on my
    fingertips.

SO, I'M ALL THE WAY TURNED ON

and there is a wide world of content about gay Black men getting
    busy
within a few keyboard strokes and mouse clicks on my PC,
where I've bookmarked the sites that don't cost nothing to preview
    three-minute clips
of them pulling, pushing, tugging, flipping, folding, holding,
    sliding, shaking,
kissing, hugging, riding, rolling, bending, rubbing, and smacking
    each other
that buffer every twenty-two seconds.

Boots is out somewhere doing whatever it is he does,
so, I log into my AIM and see a three-day-old message from Kyle
wishing me well with school, I reply, "thanks, I've got a lot of
    updates to share."
and there's a private chat request from "bigbrobrodc" with a note
    saying "sup"
that came in four hours ago.
I respond, "sup?" thinking whoever it is would respond much later,
but there is an instant response:

bigbrobrodc: sup

tonydapoet: sup?

bigbrobrodc: chillin, u?

tonydapoet: same, just got in from a poetry slam.

bigbrobrodc: oh, word, did you win Mr. Poet?

tonydapoet: I should really change my screen name lol no, I didn't win, but it was also my first time competing and I didn't know all the rules and stuff.

bigbrobrodc: that sucks. I've never met a poet before. you're like a Black William Shakespeare or something?

tonydapoet: lmao, no! I'm just me, I guess.

bigbrobrodc: so, what you about to do now?

tonydapoet: I'll probably go to bed in a few, I've got class at 8 am.

bigbrobrodc: oh, where do you go to school?

tonydapoet: my mama told me not to talk to strangers lol

bigbrobrodc: but we're already talking lol

so, how old are you?

tonydapoet: I turned 18 over the summer, but that's all I'm telling you lol what if you're a serial killer or something?

bigbrobrodc: lmao I'm not! oh damn, you can't even drink yet

tonydapoet: yeah, not legally lol

how old are you?

bigbrobrodc: I'm 22 and three months.

tonydapoet: I didn't know the months mattered after your first birthday.

bigbrobrodc: all time matters to me. so, tell me something else about yourself, it could be anything.

tonydapoet: what do you want to know?

bigbrobrodc: what are you wearing?

tonydapoet: my staple uniform: blue jeans and white T-shirt, you?

bigbrobrodc: I'm not telling you.

tonydapoet: why not?

bigbrobrodc: because you're a stranger lmao

tonydapoet: lmao no fair! but, I can tell by your screen name that you're probably in DC, and you're somebody's big brother.

bigbrobrodc: our screen names give it all away, don't they, "Tony"?

tonydapoet: ugh, you play too much. what's your name?

bigbrobrodc: I'm Wesley, but I'm not telling you my last name lol and yes, I have three little brothers.

tonydapoet: deal—and I won't tell you where I am, but I have an older sister and two stepsiblings.

bigbrobrodc: that's cool. so, now what?

tonydapoet: I don't know, I've never done this before.

bigbrobrodc: never done what?

tonydapoet: anything . . .

bigbrobrodc: you mean like, with a dude?

tonydapoet: yeah

bigbrobrodc: well, we're just chatting right? and I think that seems to be going okay.

tonydapoet: good point lol I can handle this. at least it's not a poetry slam.

bigbrobrodc: oh, so you lost, huh?

tonydapoet: lol honestly, I stunk.

bigbrobrodc: what's your stink smell like?

BEST SLEEP I'VE HAD IN A WHILE.

I was up way past midnight chatting with Wesley.
what started out as playful banter about poems, politics, and
    profanities
turned into chatter about goals, dreams, romance, and fantasies.

and we got busy without being in each other's presence.
my imagination escaped my brain and found freedom in the words
    I typed to him.
        all the things I'm scared to be specific about in my poems:
            the boys and my heartbeat
            the increasing rate of blood flowing through my body
            the private places where our aromas generate
            the flames and the fire
            going to Hell and having these desires

seems like the more I let go,
the less scared I became of myself
and so when I came to myself,
        awakening myself to Wesley's words bouncing on the screen
            at me
the Boogeyman wasn't anywhere anymore.

It was, in that moment, out of sight, out of mind.

I'mma keep Wesley as my virtual secret,
a faceless screen name of a safe and private person
who only exists when my PC is turned on

                              whenever I am turned on.
                    which is all the time.
I be awaiting the dings notifying me of new messages from him
and I despise the bloop-de-bloop sound signifying that he's logged
    out.
I be wondering where he is and what he be thinking about.
and whether my words come to mind when he's having some alone
    time.
        if he, like me, rereads the history of all our back-and-forth,
        and if he has vivid memories about what it felt like the first
            time we . . .

                              what did we do though,
        besides what I've been doing with myself for the last six years?
                        is this what first base feels like with boys?
                    is there some landing pad between where we are now
            and wherever the second space is we're supposed to go?
                        does what we did count in the book of sins
                        or did we strike some biblical balance,
            saving us both from falling into Hell's flickering flames?

        I wonder how do gay men: we: us find each other in public
    and not get punished and punched by playground bully boys.

I imagine it's a delicate dance:
probably more choreographed screenplay
than straight sexual script.
I bet it's like being real with myself
while acting to attract the eyes of somebody else
who is doing the exact same thing as me,
all while the rest of the world is watching and waiting
and judging the ways we perform ourselves
based on the presence or absence of our private parts.

I keep my lips pressed and sealed about my movements on the
    world wide web
where the boundaries are far stickier than I thought they would
    be.

privacy is survival.

NOW, I'M STUCK.

my English Comp I midterm paper is due to Prof. Latifah next
   week,
and I've been working on my thesis statement.
we've been reading *Native Son* by Richard Wright
and in our last class she asked what we thought the main point
Wright wants us to understand about the character Bigger
   Thomas:
     the root of all that love and violence, and death, and deceit,
        and fear.
whole time, this was my first time reading a work about life as a
   Black man in America,
written by someone who looked like me,
    whose parents were sharecroppers
    whose grandparents were born enslaved in Mississippi.

              Mr. Fiasco was right about MSU
        because despite all the other shit I got going on,
      I am learning a whole lot of knowledge of myself,
     especially the reasons why I be code-switching.
        this is *exactly* what I hoped to get here.
     the Boogeyman ain't welcome in these classrooms.

Prof. Latifah is at least six foot three with a voice heavier than her
    tan skin
and thicker than her long straight gray hair.
surprisingly at this HBCU, she is one of three Black professors
of the five classes I have this semester.
        the other two are from two different sides of Asia.
            I asked my academic advisor about the diversity of faculty
                here
                and he said something about supply and demand and
                    salaries and benefits.
on the first day of class Prof. Latifah said that she is only here to
    teach us
how to write   not *what* to write.
and that we *will* know the difference by the end of the semester.
she speaks essays out loud, off the top of her dome,
like some rapper freestyling in an English Comp I cipher.
and we are required to dictate all her words on the page.

she said writing is about our voice and our perspective
and it's about our readers' voices and their perspectives
and that finding a voice in the harmony between the two
is what she believes English composition is truly asking us to do.

I'm used to hearing my written voice in my poems,
but putting words on the paper for this essay ain't flowing so easy.
I need some motivation and music usually helps.

I tune my little CD boom box to 92.3 FM

and DJ Reggie Reg is playing classic hip-hop records.
I'm bopping my head and tapping my feet on the ground listening
    to
Young MC's "Bust a Move," Run DMC's "Peter Piper,"
Stetsasonic's "Talkin' All That Jazz," and De La Soul's "Me
    Myself and I."

then, he spins KRS-One's "Health, Wealth, Self"
and the lyrics say something about how emcees should have other
    ways of getting money,
instead of abusing hip-hop music
just to appease some Uncle Tom at a record company.
    and I wonder about Bigger Thomas's ways of getting money.
    how hard it was for him, a poor Black man to exist in
        Chicago in the 1930s.
    but also how easy it was for him to get busy with Mary
        Dalton *and* take her life.
        how he was victim, lover, and criminal all at the same
            time.
                and I wonder what this might mean for me:
                a poor Black gay boy in my first year of college,
            one dollar away from stealing something   if I have to,
    one playground bully boy's fist punch away from scrapping for my
                                life   if I have to.

I'm gonna argue
that Bigger Thomas was battling a Boogeyperson far more
    dangerous

than the one he probably saw in the mirror.

I'm gonna say that the history of Black people's oppression in
    America,
and the politics about our brown skin,
was the cause of Bigger Thomas's rise and fall.

I'm gonna make the case that racism and fear are first cousins.
                                    why else would that elder
        have screamed at us barefoot Black kids in church that day?
    I bet he knew all about the relationship Wright was writing about.

I'll suggest that It
is what sunk Its teeth into Bigger Thomas's neck
and dragged him around Chicago by his collar.

I'M BECOMING A POET AND A SCHOLAR.

but this ain't the different world I wanted for myself.
it's like my brain is getting smarter, but my body ain't getting free.
and it doesn't help that I don't have anyone on campus to talk to
    about any of this.
all that goes unsaid remains on repeat as background noise playing
    inside of my head.

the only person I know who is nearby is Ebby,
so I call her in her room at TU and she goes, "hey brother, what's
    going on?"
I don't hold back, "I'm not so sure I wanna be here anymore."
"um, okay, wow, is this because you and Blu broke up?" she asks.
I respond, "well, that plays a part in it, but I just don't feel like I
    belong here."
"oh Lord, Tony, what happened now? are you okay?"
                        I don't tell her about the Boogeyman
                    and how It be creeping around OC's showers.
            I don't tell her that the only time It don't show up
                    is during my private chats with Wesley.
        I don't tell her how unsafe I feel living in a residence hall
                                full of boys
who may or may not want to bench-press me up and down.

"yeah, nothing to be worried about," I say.

"I think I'm just homesick, that's all.

plus I lost a poetry slam the other night, terribly."

"wait, what?" she asks, sounding surprised.

"yeah, I bombed a whole entire performance of one of my poems."

"well, what was it about?"

"um, infinity?"

"okay, but what about infinity, Tony?"

"you know, how it lasts forever and I wanna love myself forever,

or something like that."

        I sound ridiculous, but Ebby be letting me speak.

she says, "I see, um, well, maybe you should try an open mic
    instead,"

in a tone that I want to hear as condescending, but it's actually
    soothing.

Ebby goes, "I'm on the Black Student Union (BSU) here

and we host Ebony Lounge, where lots of people get on the open
    mic

and do whatever is on their hearts,

some folks sing, some folks read poems, some folks rap,

and some folks do a whole spoken-word situation."

I go, "ooooh, like Darius Lovehall did in *Love Jones*?"

Ebby laughs and says, "yes, but without the African drums and
    jazz band.

and the best part is everybody claps for anyone who performs."

        just the kind of fuel I need.

"I don't know if we have any open mics at MSU," I say.

Ebby goes, "well, our next one is in a couple weeks and you're
     coming."

"wait, was that a question?" I ask.

"nope, I'm coming to get you and we're gonna chill here,

you'll meet some of my friends and then you're gonna spit a poem
     we're all gonna love."

"okay, I'm down," I say.

"of course you are, now go write something amazing, I've gotta
     go," she says.

"yeah, me too, peace."

I walk to the Refac thinking about what kind of poem I could
     write

that is in harmony with my voice and the audience.

I picture myself standing at a microphone on a gigantic stage

facing a crowd of bright faces and knowing my superpower is my
     spoken words,

and so my performance becomes a rescue mission.

WE ALL NEED SOME KIND OF SAVING.

I used to love coming to the Refac when the semester began,
back when I was first-year, first-generation, first-time adulting for
    real for real,
back when Blu and I were still together,
before Cubby and Dayanna started dating
before our foursome, who came here to eat together,   fell apart.
and I don't know what Blu told Dayanna
        and what Dayanna might've told Cubby
            and what Cubby might've told Bubba
                and what Bubba might've told Candy.

I hadn't seen Candy on campus all semester until a few days ago,
when I bumped into her at the bookstore.
it was a short encounter because her brother was waiting in the car,
but we planned to catch up soon and she offered me a ride to Penn
    Station
during homecoming weekend, so I could catch the MARC train
    home.

plus, my and Cubby's schedules don't match up enough for us to
    see each other,

except in Business Orientation class,
but I (intentionally) arrive late and sit in the back,
so I can avoid talking to him about OC, Blu, and the Boogeyman.

whenever I eat here, I walk to one of the tables in the back
where people who don't want to be bothered go sit by themselves
    and eat in silence.
I crush my chicken fingers and cheese fries and go back to my
    room.

Boots is on the third floor playing spades with the guy from NYC
who snuck in a George Foreman Grill.
I am about to log on to AIM and see if there are any messages
    from Wesley,
when Calvin comes knocking on my door.
he's wearing a loose-fitted ribbed white tank top
and a pair of wrinkled eggshell thermal pants with the soft waffle
    stitching.
                                        at least it's something.
"yo, T, what you got going on tonight?"
"I ain't doing shit but hanging in my room."
"you wanna go to Dave and Buster's with me and some of my
    friends?"
"I would, but I'm flat broke, man.
I can barely afford to pay attention," chuckling off my
    embarrassment.
"oh, I hear you, it be like that sometimes."
"thanks for asking me though, Calvin, I appreciate it."

"no problem, brotha."

I close the door and as soon as AIM connects,
there are loud knocks firing at rapid speed on my door and
    someone is yelling, "Tony!"
I yell out, "this better be the police!"   it is not.
it is Calvin, MJ, Auggie, and Chris: a few guys in OC who I've
    spoken to a few times
when we cross paths in the hall.
they be in Calvin's room listening to hip-hop music sometimes.
    I can hear them down there rapping and freestyling.
    I be wanting to tell them I'm not a rapper,
    but Gary said poetry and rap go together,
    which means I could *at least* write them some better bars.
    I be wanting to join in their cipher,
    but I don't feel safe engaging with them like that.

these fellas are all stacked in height order looking down at me.
Calvin is holding a black snapback cap upside down in his left
    hand
and it has about $22 worth of crumpled-up dollar bills.
he says, "*we* got you, bro, now let's go!"
I show my first real smile in a while and agree to join them
with a plan to just play it straight.

AND I DO A GREAT JOB TOO:

I shoot basketballs inside of impossibly placed hoops,
and slide hockey pucks on slick faux ice that land inside of side
    slots,
that make neon blue lights fly around in a plastic bubble.
I toss tiny wooden balls up slanted planes
that fall into concentric circles worth between 5 to 100 points,
and drive simulated race cars that spit out the tickets
that we trade in at the prize store,
where I choose a pencil that has a jelly monster
jiggling on the end where an eraser should be,
and a large pack of Now and Laters.

we eat slices of pepperoni pizza from the same pie
that has a crispy hard crust and not nearly enough tomato sauce,
and drink flat ginger ale from the endless flowing fountain,
and pat each other on the back,
and laugh in each other's faces,
and smile into each other's spaces.

I do not think about being gay until we get back to the OC
and Calvin goes, "ah, man, that was a blast, did you have fun, T?"
"I damn sure did, we'll definitely have to do that again."

I mean it but can't afford it.

"well, what are you about to do now?" he asks.

"Boots ain't here, so, I'll probably study for a lil bit before taking
    my ass to bed."

which is partially true.
I plan on chatting with Wesley.

Calvin says, "I'm about to go chill with this girl in Harper-
    Tubman
who got a way to get niggas in there.
her roommate is phat as a mug too, dawg,
you wanna come with me and we can all kick it?"

I blink. I catch. I stop breathing.

I can't imagine what Calvin's reaction would be
if I tell him that I'm gay,
but that I ain't too sure about it yet
because I've never actually gotten busy with another boy before.

I don't tell him that I know that he ain't gay.
and that I ain't hitting on him or nothing,
or trying to convert the orientation of his sexual compass,
and that I'm just tryna figure it all out by myself
without provoking playground bully boys to beat me up.

my stomach hurts.

"oh, nah Calvin, that's all you, brotha,
I'mma be in here with my head in these books." I manage to laugh.

then he smiles at me,
as if he is the proud papa of the nerdy boy standing in front of
    him,
instead of the straight man I am trying to be.

Calvin makes a peaceful exit down the hall,
dropping one of his Dave and Buster's tickets on the floor.
I don't tell him to turn around so that he can pick up a memento
from the best night that I've had since being at MSU.
instead, I place the memory in my pocket
and decide that Calvin can no longer be my boy-friend.
and so, I dig a deeper well into the mud that I've made out of
    myself,
        further burying my hermit crab shell.

TALKING TO MYSELF ON THE PAGE

when I'm not in class, I've spent most of my time barricaded in my
    room
writing poems to fight the Boogeyman,
and coming up with a piece to share at Ebony Lounge tonight.

I've been writing something different from my hidden poems.
in this piece, I imagined myself performing it for an audience,
and so, instead of asking myself questions about who I am,
I am asking myself: what is it that I want my poetry to do?

the words took shape on the page as they would in spoken form
        something inspired by Nikki Giovanni's poem "Sound in
            Space"
            where there is a stream of consciousness that also tells a
                story
            and it has rhythm and rhymes occasionally
            and metaphors that don't bend the mind too far.
                it's one of Blu's favorites.

this is the longest poem I've ever written
and I feel like I could've kept on going, but I needed to stop.

there's still words left to be said though.
I've been reading it over and over in my head and in the mirror,
    softly,
just becoming familiar with how I sound saying all of this out
    loud.
I wish I could memorize it, or maybe freestyle,
or do whatever it is that Darius Lovehall did in his "Blues for
    Nina."
but I print my poem out, fold it up, and put it in my pocket for
    tonight.

TU's campus appears twice the size of MSU.
Ebby and I meet up with her friends Pootah, Tee, Tisha, and
    Chanel.
I am the only Black boy walking with a group of Black girls on a
    college campus
that resembles the book cover with all the college rankings.
Ebby is giving me a brief tour: "we have about 14,000 undergrad
    students total
and about 10,500 of them are white kids."
Pootah says, "yeah, I think *we* make up close to 1,300 of the Black
    ones."

                    whole time, I'm fascinated to hear them discuss
                what number of a few hundred each of them represent
            on a campus where there are more than a few thousand people.

"that's the Smith building over there
and across the street is the Center for the Arts.

we are headed to the University Union, our main student center."
Ebby points directly ahead and I am surprised to see
a swarm of Black people with different shades of brown skin
rushing through the front entrance to the University Union
and beelining their way into a ballroom where there is a
    microphone standing on an empty stage.

Ebby grabs my hand and pulls me inside
and over to meet the host of Ebony Lounge, Rebecca.
she is wearing thigh-high leather boots
and a formfitting jersey dress and mini denim jacket
and holding a clipboard with a sign-up sheet.
"hey girl, this is my brother, Tony, I was telling you about him the
    other day."
"oh hey, brother Tony!" Rebecca says with a giant smile.
"you getting on the mic or what?"

                                            my stomach hurts.
I hesitate, "I don't know, I mean I *did* bring a poem
but don't be performing my stuff like that."

Ebby says all in one breath, "first of all, Tony, why are you
    playing?
second of all, you know you got all the bars.
third of all, you told me the other day
that you were gonna write something to perform tonight.
don't tell me that I drove all the way to MSU
to pick your Black behind up from OC
just so that you could attend Ebony Lounge

and sit in the corner like some quiet church mouse.
so, whatever you got in your notebook for tonight
that is what you're going to do.
Rebecca, put Tony on the list."

I do not protest.
we go sit down a few rows in front of the stage
where I'm fiddling with the poem in my pocket.

OPEN MICS AIN'T A SLAM.

ain't no judges, scorecards, or rules for rounds.
it's just a bunch of us in here feeling the vibe.
the lights are dim and there is a DJ in the corner who just finished
    playing
"Outside Your Door" by Meshell Ndegeocello.
Rebecca walks to the standing microphone
like a strong and hungry lion approaches a soft grazing gazelle
that's about to be chewed into bits.
and she literally attacks us all
with a love poem about some ignorant-ass guy she used to date.
apparently, he lied to her about the true nature of his heart,
so she metaphorically bites into his chest,
making sure that he too gets torn apart.

Rebecca just made Ebony Lounge feel like church.
we've all been moved in this crowd to clap our hands,
snap our fingers, stand up, and shout out praises.
"thanks, y'all, I am Rebecca, and am serving as your host this
    evening.
welcome to Ebony Lounge everybody!"
the entire room erupts in cheers.

I look at Ebby and say, "damn, that's how you open a show!"
she goes, "oh, you ain't seen nothing yet.
we've got a lot of talented poets at TU and Rebecca is top tier."

Rebecca says, "as you all know, we would not be here if it were not
    for
the original BSU members who stormed President Fisher's office
    in 1970
as a protest for racial equality on campus,
and demanded that Black students have a space where
we can freely, loudly, and clearly express our voices.
can we get a 'one time' for the ancestors?"
    we all go, "one time!"
Rebecca says, "Asé."
                        whole time, I'm shocked that we can be *this* Black at a
                            Predominantly White Institution (PWI).
                                and the Boogeyman don't show up.

"I am so glad that you all could be here tonight.
I know it's Friday and you could be anywhere,
but you chose to kick it with us at Ebony Lounge.
and on behalf of *your* BSU, thanks for coming.
we're going to get right to it and bring up our very first poet.
he currently attends MSU and is the brother of my homegirl Ebby,
who many of you know from BSU.
y'all, he's already told me that he is a little nervous,
but we only do love over here at Ebony Lounge, right?"
the crowd responds, "yeah!"
"so, let's all give Tony Keith some TU love as he makes his way to

the mic!"
I am full.

I am not as afraid as I thought I would be.
the crowd is looking at me, eager to hear what it is that I have to
    say,
and I actually want to tell them this poem.

"peace everyone, my name is Tony, I'm from DC and yeah, um,
    I'mma poet.
I wrote this piece a few nights ago while thinking about my
    relationship
with poetry and what I understand God to be.
that probably sounds weird, but I am really tryna figure it all out,
so don't y'all judge me too hard, okay?" I laugh off my nerves.
Rebecca shouts out, "no disclaimers, speak your truth, poet!"

I pull the poem out of my pocket, breathe in deep, close my eyes,
    and exhale:

I think, I beat, and I purge all thoughts and words
        on this quirky qwerty keyboard
        wearing pieces of paper like it's denim,
    canvas shoes and a crisp white cotton T-shirt,
    pounding on plastic letters in a wiry rhythm
        that no one can hear but me.

In my head it sounds like a musical instrumental
        laced with sycophantic subliminals

to get God inside my poetry.

you see, I don't need traditional Black church homiletics
and Rev., Dr., Bishop to evangelize and use prophetics
cuz I can shout on my own
simply by capitalizing my letters
and using exclamations in my poems,
hoping to free those that read 'em
listen to 'em and recite 'em like they wrote 'em.

I'm in search of contemplation.
I'm seeking separation from mainstream artistic expression
that lacks depth and dimensions.
I want my writing to be multi-layered, multi-leveled,
multi-cultural
and able to be multi-plied infinite times.

yes, I'm seeking exponential creativity
that continues to build upon its power until the end of time,
even if that time is infinity
just immortalize my shit and put everything I ever wrote
on my tombstone when you bury me,
and make sure the hole is deep enough to carry me,
and you invoke the spirit of my poems when you read my
eulogy.

I want to be known as that artsy-fartsy intellect
who believed there is power in words,
and that I not only cared for what I said,

but took responsibility for those that heard
whether or not I pissed them off
or convinced them to change the world.

let them know that sometimes I got tired,
and that sometimes I got weary
but I kept writing even when my vision was blurry,
and I couldn't see what was in front of me.

I kept writing when people told me to sit still.
they'd say, "boy, grass never grows under your feet"
but that's cuz I'm too busy climbing uphill.

tell them that I didn't have time to rest
until the rest of my poems were written
but I couldn't stop writing, so none of my poems have endings,
just transitions between new beginnings
and space savers while refilling ink in my pen again
or checking my dictionary for definitions,
my thesaurus for synonyms,
and asking my Pop-Pop to recount his history
and teach me his wisdom
and if I needed to sleep and dream just to recharge my system,
or if I need to take a moment, set my pen on record,
sip some coffee, and just listen . . .

and for me, listening ain't always easy.
I always got too much to say
and taking pauses for others never really appeased me,

it wasn't until my search for God that I found humility.

but to be clear,
I ain't scared to write a poem about my ashy knuckles
and my humble, buckling knees
or stand tall on stages, grab my dick,
and tell the world to hum on deez.
I ain't afraid to write a poem about my spit being so hot
that it boils at zero degrees.
I ain't scared to perform in places with Amen corners
where people are screaming "God bless" me, like I sneezed,
or to write poems at the wishes of others and say,
"God grant them these.
cuz these be your people trying to get to you
by getting through me."
but I'm not a medium, I actually wear a small;
a powerful lil poet not standing very tall,
and yet still trying to acquire it all.

y'all I'm in search of contemplation.
I'm trying to write some haikus
that I can put in the curriculum in high schools
that get students to contemplate on whether getting high is cool

yo, I wanna think myself to literary breakthrough.
write a poem so long
I'll have to give my audience a break halfway through.
so y'all gonna have to come back later on
if you wanna hear this knucklehead spit part two.

I BELONG HERE.

I take a slight bow, say thank you, and all I can hear is the crowd
  screaming:
"whoa!" "ay!" "c'mon!" "yes!" "okay, poet!" "Tony!" "wow!" "oh my
  God!"
Snap! Clap! Snap! Clap! Snap! Clap! Snap! Clap! Snap! Clap!
Rebecca approaches me onstage where my voice
is still climbing down from atop the standing microphone
and gives me a long and warm embrace.
she says, "y'all, please give it up again for *our* brotha, Tony the
  poet."

now, I can't stop thinking about all the things I'd do different next
  time:
      connect with my story, memorize my words
      practice my performance, slow down my stanzas
      focus on the audience, enjoy being in the moment
      develop an arc for my poem, speak clearly as myself
      be intense and theatrical and funny and confident
        all the things hip-hop is teaching me
        all the things English Comp I is teaching me
        all the things GLC youth choir is teaching me

saying all that out loud made me want to write more poems
to move the crowds as a college student poet,
but MSU and my poems don't fit together.
which is what I'm chatting with Tiffy about on AIM.

tiffy_writes: so glad to hear you're getting closer to your Darius Lovehall moment sweetie lol. it sucks that you're not having the best time at MSU though.

tonydapoet: yeah, I just feel like this school might not be the right fit for me. you know, I didn't see any colleges at all before I applied, right? shit, I barely got in here lol

tiffy_writes: oh, I remember lol I applied to like nine different places lol 3 reach, 3 target, and 3 safety—I wanted options! Lol

tonydapoet: oh, damn, that makes sense. I don't know if MSU would've been one of my target schools, but I guess being here was the only way I'd figure that out, huh?

tiffy_writes: couldn't you transfer to another school?

tonydapoet: I think so, but I don't know how all that works with credits and stuff. I know that my math class doesn't count for anything this semester.

tiffy_writes: got it. have you spoken to Blu at all since you broke up?

tonydapoet: nah, not really. she got her own group of friends now and I don't really talk to Cubby anymore. have you spoken with her?

tiffy_writes: nope, we haven't been in touch much since graduation.

tiffy_writes: when's the next time you're coming home?

tonydapoet: maybe this weekend, I don't wanna be here for homecoming. there's no one to really hang with but Boots and you know how he is.

tiffy_writes: lol I love my roomie Kelli, you should come visit us!

tonydapoet: bet!

I'M OUT OF HERE.

it's MSU's homecoming, and everyone has been bitten by the
  school spirit bear bug,
and I want nothing more than to get away from OC.
my routine as of late is wake up, go to class, go to my room,
go to the Refac, go back to my room, ignore Boots's shenanigans,
shit, shower, study, sorta kinda sleep, wash, rinse, and repeat.

classes are canceled, but I slid my midterm paper under Prof.
  Latifah's office door.
I am so grateful that Candy ain't ask me for a single dollar or dime
to drop me off at Penn Station just in time to catch my MARC
  train.
truth is, Ma's new town house is only forty-five minutes away,
but I ain't been there at all this semester because I can't pay for any
  form of transportation.
I've been saving this $5 to pay for this ticket.

I walk quickly toward the train car and grab the first open
  window seat.
I stuff my suitcase and duffle in the top rack and place my book
  bag underneath my legs.

I reach in my right front pocket and pull out the Dave and Buster's
    ticket
laugh quietly to myself before wiping away a tear.

I don't tell Ma about Calvin when I wrap my arms around her
    shoulders
and squeeze her tight to my chest in the parking lot at Seabrook
    station,
        she's driving a new car.
I don't tell her that I don't eat regularly
or that I'm comfortable being alone with my PC that is serving
    multiple purposes.
instead, I tell her about my stellar grades, the spoken essays in
    Prof. Latifah's class,
Ebby and TU and performing at Ebony Lounge,
and my buddy night out with the fellas,
and funny stories about Boots, just being himself.

she tells me all about the staff changes on her job
and about the town house she just bought
and about how much she loves her new neighbors
and how quiet the neighborhood is
and how she loves being a homeowner

Ma's house is six doors down from Auntye P's place.
my room is tiny, which I guess makes sense because I don't live here,
but there isn't any space for me to comfortably extend my growing
    legs.

while at MSU, I grew those three inches that I thought I grew
    before,
none of my clothes fit me right anymore.
Tamu's room is next door and twice the size.

it feels great to have my own space and a separate bathroom to use
    again
even if it's just for a few days.
and it smells like fresh warm laundry and the lavender carpet
    powder
Ma sprinkles before she vacuums.
and I can hear her in the kitchen, taking out the pots and pans
about to prepare the first homecooked meal I've had in months.

best of all, ain't no other boys living in here.
I don't have to avoid looking at sweaty chests and handsome
    faces
and hairy happy trails leading toward anyone else's private places.
I don't have to watch my back in the shower.
I don't have to listen to Boots inhale the holes in his lungs every
    half an hour.

Ma yells upstairs, "you have some mail, baby, I left it on your
    dresser."
after putting my first load of laundry into a machine that doesn't
    require quarters,
I open the envelope from Student Visa with my brand-new credit
    card inside.

I peel the sticky part off the back, sign my name, and drive Ma's
    car to Old Navy.
I confirm with my manager that I can come back in December
and then I charge up $255.97 worth of clothes to help me survive
the rest of my first year at MSU.

my next stop is to get a haircut from Wayne at the Shop.

BARBERSHOPS ARE TRICKY.

it's the only place in my world where I both love all that goes on,
but am terrified to engage in the hypermasculine banter
because I don't know enough sports stats, athlete names, trivial
    plays on the field,
team positions, court boundaries, or complicated referee calls for a
    review of the game.

and I don't want to risk anyone calling me a punk, pussy, or
    faggot.

I started going to the Shop in middle school when Pop-Pop passed
    away.
we couldn't afford a barber, so Ma took my hair care into her own
    hands.
        bought a set of discount store clippers
        and with no preparation but prayer slid buzzing sharp metal
            blades
        across my scalp with the number one guard: the *only* barrier
            size she used.
        she did not buy trimmers, which meant I had no shape-up.

so, in addition to being bullied because I was too soft and skinny
my mother sent me to school with homemade haircuts that always
     drew attention.
in sixth grade, at my request to look cooler, she attempted to give
     me a high-top fade
by cutting the southern hemisphere smooth enough to expose the
     skin,
and then used her faithful number one guard on the northern part
     of my scalp
she didn't know how to blend the hair together
and I was forced to pretend as if there was some gradation
near an equator that did not exist.

I wore a bowl-shaped plot of dry land until Pop told Ma
that I should go to the Shop where Uncle Lamont,
one of his Masonic brothers, is a master barber.

Uncle Lamont is a tall, slim man with pale lemon skin,
a thin goatee, high-top fade, who wore a pair of black eyeglasses
that looked exactly like the ones Malcolm X is wearing
in the poster next to the large oval mirror in his booth,
surrounded by pictures of his wife and children.

I am unsure what financial arrangements Ma made with him back
     then
but he kept asking me to sweep up the hair falling to the floor,
and to get him black coffee from the corner store,
and restack the magazines in the order they were before

he allowed his customers to enter the front doors.
the Shop was a large leap from Pop-Pop's dining room,
where it was no one but us and the rhubarbs and the rain that ain't
    hurt.

my barber, Wayne, is from Jamaica and has a slightly crooked cool
    smile.
he started working at the Shop after doing his apprenticeship here.
I *only* go to him because of his consistently flawless fades
with the extra crispy, tight, straight-lined edges
which he carves around each corner of our craniums.

I take a deep breath and close my eyes while he scrapes my scalp
    cool,
causing layers of my hair to fall to the same floor I used to sweep
    as a kid.
    it's as if all the stress and worry from the last few months
      are being mowed to their death by jumping off the cliff that
        is my crown.

I listen as Wayne, Uncle Lamont, and some of their customers
debate their knowledge of sports and politics, and sex and
    marriage,
and church and hard work, and education, and money, and health,
    and raising young kings.
    trying to prove themselves right by adjusting their volume,
      treble, and bass
    in a battle of wits with their tongues.

and anyone who enters the war was fair game for a verbal
  slaughter,
regardless of age, except the one elder who was present.
Uncle Lamont says that bald-headed old Black man comes twice a
  week
just to sit still in their barbershop all day, play chess, drink coffee,
  and talk shit.

no one is arguing with him until one of the customers calls him
  "grandpa so-and-so,"
and the OG, wise and reserved as a Buddhist monk meditating on
  mountaintops,
cuts that poor man down to a smaller size by speaking one cryptic
  line,
which still don't make sense, but ain't worth fussing with him
  about:
    "boy, I was gutting fish with my wisdom teeth
    and boiling their eyeballs in raccoon oil
    before the day your daddy realized that he ain't have two left
      feet
    left in his mouth to tickle your mama with at night."

the only thing I know is safe to do in here is laugh when everyone
  else does,
so I join in while Wayne finishes up my cut.
I look in the mirror and I feel fresh and clean
and I smell like Egyptian-musk alcohol wipes and coconut oil hair
  spray.

I wonder if now, I could describe what I look like to Wesley.

I try not to look at myself too long.
wouldn't want anyone to think I'm caring too much about my
    appearance.
      or Uncle Lamont might ask how the girls are treating me on
        campus
        or Wayne might ask me what's up with the girl I was
          dating in high school.
           or they might ask me what girl I'm about to go see.

and with a credit card and three dollars in cash to pay for my cut
I don't protest when Wayne lets me slide out of the Shop for free.

THIS IS A DIFFERENT WORLD

it's good to see Tiffy.
    I've missed all her glittery butterfly purpleness.
she lives in a coed residence hall where boys and girls live on
    alternate floors,
all with unlimited access to each other.
I am captivated by her room,
which is complete with mini fridge, microwave, teakettle,
    photographs pinned to the walls, string lights, clean carpet,
    bookcases, shelves full of snacks and shit.
plus it smells like a warm bowl of honeysuckle and rose water
    soup.
                          this makes OC look like the slums.

we are sipping instant coffee from Styrofoam cups with the little
    ridges,
she didn't have any milk or sugar so we improvised
by scraping the cream from the middle of chocolate sandwich
    cookies
into boiling hot brown water.
      we stirred all that thick white syrupy stuff
        until most of it dissolved into tiny clumps that taste terribly
           satisfying.

we are with her roommate Kelli—a Black girl with clear brown
     eyes,
who is a ginormous ball of cheerleading energy,
and their friend Errica—a sassy and petite woman with
     sandalwood skin
who is comfortably displaying her bodacious boobs in a men's
     dress shirt
with the top three buttons undone and the collar spread out.

we're all discussing Errica's cleavage and caffeinating
before we attend a step show at the Nyumburu Cultural Center,
which they said is UMD's freedom house for Black students on
     campus,
created by their BSU as a response to racial protests
on the steps of the main Administration Building in the 1960s.

when I asked why a Black cultural center is at a PWI,
Errica responded, "well, where else on this campus am I gonna be
     able to see myself
reflected on these white-ass academic walls."

                    I think about how I see myself every day at MSU,
                    and how it ain't my Blackness or my brilliance
                    that's reflecting in the Boogeyman's face,
                    it's the fact that I'm poor and gay
                    and can't be free where I'm at.

                    if I were to transfer to a predominantly white school,
                    I'd definitely be a part of the BSU,

seems like that's where the belonging is for Black students
who ain't a part of the majority.

Tiffy says, "I see white people here, but I don't know
if we *exactly see* each other, you know what I'm saying?"
we all say, "absolutely."

it's almost 10 p.m. but UMD's campus is as bright as noon smack-
dab in midsummer.
there are tall and fully functioning light poles firmly cemented in
clean concrete,
and blue emergency booths with dial pad and speaker,
and lit pathways along the sidewalk that leads to Denton Hall,
which is open for something called "late night."
Kelli asks, "you want something to eat, Tony?"
besides the lumps of chocolate cookie cream,
I haven't considered the fact my stomach has been growling for
hours.
I'm used to not eating regularly, but I don't dare tell Kelli that,
instead, I start patting the pockets of my new jeans, "oh, I don't
have any cash."

Tiffy says, "that's okay, you can use some of my points."
"I can do what?" I ask, with my face pulled into itself.
"oh, Daddy made sure that he got me the supreme meal plan when
I registered.
it's basically unlimited amounts of food and I never eat enough
so my points keep on accumulating.
I'm tryna avoid that first-year fifteen,"

grabbing skin around her abdomen.
"I know that's right, girl," Errica says, and they all laugh.

whole time, I'm thinking about what I'm gonna eat on Sunday
    night
if I don't get to the Refac before 7:30 p.m.
I don't protest any longer and eagerly accept this divine invitation
to eat my portion of their collective unused points.
        I am filling up: literally, piling my cafeteria tray with shrimp
            scampi, linguini,
        bruschetta, shredded roast chicken fajitas with fresh
            guacamole,
        and jalapeño honey butter corn bread cupcakes
        topped with maple cream cheese frosting.

I also learn they have a free campus shuttle run by UMD students
that goes in a loop inside of campus and makes stops all over,
including commuter students who live in the surrounding area.
Tiffy says she heard sometimes white students be really drunk and
    annoying
after a long night of partying on Frat Row, so she don't ride it.

we arrive for the step show, and it seems like every Black student
    is here.
all of a sudden, there's a loud call whistling through the air
I look down in the amphitheater and there's a fraternity
dressed in black T-shirts, camouflage pants, and black boots
and they're clapping and stomping,

and making sharp movements with their legs and arms,
and wrists and fists, and synchronizing how they jump in the air.
   I am in awe watching them freestyle-stroll through a cipher
   with choreographed lines and circles shaped by vibrations
      coming from
the hip-hop, R&B, funk, and soul music blasting from
   gigantic portable speakers:

"Mic Checka" by Das EFX
"Candy" by Cameo
"Atomic Dog" by George Clinton
"Rosa Parks" by Outkast
"Set It Off" by Strafe
"Got to Be Real" by Cheryl Lynn

I wonder if perhaps I could transfer here.
if perhaps Ma could let me live in my tiny room.
if perhaps I could catch the free shuttle.
if perhaps I could eat my girl-friend's unused meal points.
then perhaps I could reduce my college costs.
then perhaps I could pay my credit card bill.

I'M OUT OF HERE.

I was chatting with Wesley last night,
telling him how I don't need the stars to fall any harder from the
   sky
to understand that I can't fully be myself at MSU
and that it makes sense to try and transfer to UMD, where I got
   better survival options.

he told me that if I were to move back to PG,
we'd have to find a way to meet each other somehow.
I think I scared him a little because I didn't respond right away.
took me a while to figure out what I wanted to say,
               I was thinking about the fact that the Boogeyman
                              be moving with me
         and how I will still need to fight that battle living with Ma.
my response was, "let's just leave it in God's hands."
Wesley wished me luck and said he'd pray for me.

predicting *that* kind of future with myself in it is frightening
because that means I'm not just gay in the world wide web kind of
   way,
but I am also out and I guess proud about it too,

which ain't my truth at all.

        I don't want to be gay, but it's never been a choice,
    and I don't know how to explain that to anyone but Wesley.

I imagine what it'd be like seeing him in real life:
we'd decide to meet at a water fountain on a warm sunny day
and sit next to each other, but don't speak right away,
then one of us will decide it's time to say the other's name out
    loud,
and wait for the words to land on the right person,
and they will, which makes us both laugh
and then, I draw a blank . . .
there's no movies with characters who act out scenes
that explain how gay men be themselves and be with each other,
    especially in public.
so I can't picture what's supposed to happen.

and I can't force the stars to align in my favor.
I can only hope that the faith I pulled on to get to MSU in the
    first place
will also show up in full glory when the time comes again for my
    world to pivot.
I'm accustomed to change, so I can handle it.

so I don't hold back revising my personal statement in my
    application.
    I tell UMD I want to be closer to home.
    I tell them I saw Nyumburu and attended a step show.

I tell them I know all about the history of the BSU.

I tell them it's not a lot of students that look like me on their campus.

I tell them I'm a first-generation college student seeking a better fit.

WISHING FOR DIVINE INTERVENTION.

I turn myself into a hermit crab the rest of this semester,
burying myself deeper in the mud at OC,

    surviving on private chats with Wesley about meeting in
      person

      dreaming in AIM messages to Tiffy about changing
        schools,

        ignoring Boots's disastrous commentary

          dodging Cubby on campus

      believing Blu is happier without me

and spending time at TU with Ebby and her girl-friends.
tonight we're going to College Night at DC Live,
it's eighteen to party, but twenty-one to drink,
we just gotta show our school IDs and wear a neon wrist band all
    night.
I got ready in my room and walked on over to Auntye P's,
well dressed in my best new debt.

Ebby and her girl-friends are walking around sans shirts,
applying their makeup, flat ironing their hair, changing outfits,
    swapping stilettos,
and nary one of them blinked an eye or batted a freshly curled-up

eyelash
when they removed, rearranged, and put on their bras in front of me.
I missed getting hit with Tee's right nipple,
after ducking before her boobs missed their moment to flop in my
   face.

                              although I might be gay, I love boobs,
                         just not in the getting busy kind of way.

we arrive at the club and I am the only boy amongst the group.
   I believe that they are all absolutely okay with our platonic
      arrangement too,
   I don't mind just being their boy-friend.

DC Live has three floors and three DJs
who are blending, scratching, and layering some of my favorite
   songs:
                     "Thong Song" by Sisqo
              "Always on Time" by Ja Rule and Ashanti
                     "Vivrant Thing" by Q-Tip
                   "The Bud" by Huck-A-Bucks
                  "Dolly My Baby" by Super Cat
I become the soft part in the middle of my girl-friend cookie
   sandwich
waving my hands high in the air while they circle around me,
bouncing their big ole butts and boobs
and rotating their legs, arms, shoulders all up on me.
they say they love dancing with me

'cause I don't be tryna grab no parts of them,
I don't be tryna pull on none of their limbs,
I don't be tryna push myself through my pants into them.

I just keep my hands to myself, until the DJ spins "Da Butt" by
    E.U.,
and Ebby signals that it's time for them to back all of themselves
    up on me
as I pretend their bottoms are turntables
and I'm scratching and mixing all of them around.

I look up and see all these Black men watching me dance with all
    these women.
and I bet they're calling me a faggot under their breath.
I bet they're laughing at me because I ain't getting busy with them
    for real for real.
I bet they think I've been trying to lure some straight man into a
    trap,
where he winds up with his hands around my waist without free
    will.
      truth is: I don't want to be with them in the way I want
        Wesley.

we all decide to take a break and I gotta pee,
I go in the men's room and discover it's got the urinals sticking out
    of the wall
instead of the ones that are bolted to the floor.
and there's absolutely no barricade between the bowls that form a

    private structure
in between you and the next person who is also peeing.

to be clear, I ain't tryna get busy with boys in bathrooms,
it's just that trying to pee next to strange people
who are also spraying their urine in their own bowl,
while all our private parts are out there exposed,
makes my internal rhythm anxious.
     I shared a bathroom with Tamu for eighteen years
     and so I know to close the door and pee privately,
     and make sure to lower the seat back,
     and wipe the edges around the toilet with tissue
     because, for real for real, my aim be a lil off when I shake
        sometimes.

I end up standing at that urinal for like twenty-six seconds
holding my stuff and pointing it toward the target,
listening to other boys wait, let go, and leave.
I take several sighs before saying, "I thought I had to go" quietly
    enough
so that the other boys peeing around me know
that I ain't creeping, controlling, or standing guard,
I just misunderstood my body for a moment.

I zip myself back together, wash my hands, exit stage left,
and wait until we leave to release my wet waste out back
in the dark alley with dancing rats,
and up against a brick wall near smelly dumpsters,
because somehow that was more humane.

I LOVE A GOOD PARTY.

I am looking at the Polaroid we all took tonight
with my girl-friends surrounding me like a rapper on a CD cover,
except we are all clothed and platonically touching.

I am expecting to come back to a quiet town house,
but everything is buzzing in here.
all the lights are on and Tamu is hunched over the dining room table,
crying as if she is birthing pain from her back,
which Ma is rubbing and patting aggressively,
      trying to soothe her firstborn baby singing repeatedly, "it's
        okay, Boobie."
she is in her extra-long nightshirt and her eyes look a little puffy,
which means she must've awoken from her sleep
to attend to her child's weeping and wailing.
my teenage lil cousin Tosh Mosh is here too,
and she is watching the local news channel.

I rush over to them.
"what's wrong? what happened? why are you crying?"
my big sister looks up at me with a gallon of salt water dried to her
    face
and she can barely breathe in between her words,

"he's dead, Tony.
	they shot him.
		they killed him.
			he ain't do nothing.
				he ain't have no gun in his hands.
					I held him in my arms."

"what? who? where? huh?"
Tamu can't say it, and so Ma does,
"baby, a PG police officer killed Gary tonight."
I blink. I catch. I stop breathing.

this sharp thing stings deep inside	my heart breaks.

I'm hearing Gary's voice inside my head as Tosh Mosh explains
what they're saying is written in the police report:

she says that police spokesperson Lt. Andrew Ellis said something
	about
two off-duty PG County officers were guarding the party
where she, Tamu, and Gary were some of twenty-five people
involved in a series of fights.

then somebody told one of da officers that there were weapons
inside of somebody's car,
which prompted the officer to request some assistance.

so, a third officer pulls up to da car where da weapon is supposed

to be,
and that must be where Gary is at,
because when he orders errbody in the car to put their hands up,
Gary gets out.

she says Gary approached the officer, who has his gun drawn
and pointed somewhere near his body.

Tosh Mosh says Lt. Andrew Ellis said that Gary's hands got on to
    da officer's gun
and dat they engaged in a vurry intense struggle.

then, the off-duty officer who requested assistance
runs over to break up the tussle
and with his gun fired one bullet into Gary's chest,
causing him to lose his grip   and put his hands in the air.

at 2:59 a.m. on November 27, 1999,
Gary Albert Hopkins Jr. died at Doctors Hospital in
Lanham, MD.

Lt. Andrew Ellis didn't say he was nineteen.
he didn't say he was Black.
he didn't say his life mattered to anybody.
he didn't say he was a DuVal High graduate.
he didn't say he transferred to PG Community College
after spending his first year at Johnson C. Smith University,
he didn't say he was a poet who rapped and rhymed on beat.

he didn't say he was homecoming king.
he didn't say he made the whole cafeteria feel like love.
he didn't say he made up the word "misphlopotant."
he didn't say dat Gary said misphlopotant means
"those moments when sumthn just ain't right."

"dis some misphlopotant shit!" I scream out.

Gary's mama says they're going to trial.
Gary's mama says her son's death is a senseless killing.
Gary's mama says there's no transparency from those we pay to
protect us.
Gary's mama says systemic racism runs deep in the veins of the
police force.
Gary's mama says to tell the world to say his name.

SUMMER 2000

SURVIVING MY FIRST YEAR IS A BLURRY DREAM.

turning into a hermit crab and burying myself deeper in the OC
    mud
was a great strategy for remaining invisible on MSU's campus.
no one knew who I was, nor did they ask about me.
I finished the fall semester with a 3.7 GPA,
and was inducted into the first-year student Honor Society.
       I didn't go to the ceremony, just had them mail my certificate
         to Ma.

I got a 2.8 in the spring and that's only because Dr. Grimaces gave
    me a D
in his Computer Applications class.
 I still don't know why that big ole Black man, his sassy-ass attitude,
      and bland bald face, and dry Q-tip hair, and gigantic thick feet,
          decided that he ain't like me because I didn't understand
             the difference between a micro-byte and a micro-bit.
               I wanted to tell him that I ain't give a micro-shit,
                 but Ma would be disappointed if she found out.

I found solace in Ebby and Tiffy, and of course, Wesley:
who I've been chatting with almost every day for the past few weeks,

mostly getting to know each other better and without hiding
    information.
I learned that he's from southern Mississippi:
a self-defined church boy, who sings tenor too.
he works a full-time government job, drives his own car,
and lives with his sister in Clinton, MD.
        Wesley says that he ain't out to his family,
        but he is out in the Black gay DC scene,
        which he says is its own bubble of brown skin men
        who all know each other in one way or another,
                he keeps saying he'll explain that part to me later.

Wesley and I only know what we look like based on our Yahoo
    profile pictures.
I purchased a web camera and uploaded a headshot of myself
    sitting at my PC
showing my bright white straight smile, and slim titanium oval-
    shaped eyeglasses,
he has a picture of himself singing on a microphone,
but I can't tell who is in the audience or where he is,
but I assume he's singing for Sunday service somewhere.

we have those cute little flirtatious moments where we'll say
    things like:
"whatever, babe," "you know you want me to," "good night, sexy,"
"you miss me?" "I'm ready whenever you are," "prove it."
my buddy lists and gay getting busy website bookmarks have
    grown exponentially.
and since the Y2K bug ain't really bite nobody,

I joined the world of Black folks connecting on BlackPlanet.com,
where my screen name is "Poetician,"
      which I'm sure has some Webster's dictionary definition,
         but I was tryna be clever with my wordplay,
         because I'm kinda like a poet-magician
            performing tricks on the page and the stage.

I be logging in chat rooms on CollegeClub.com
where I've made virtual friends with Black gay college men
who live in Miami, FL; Ithaca, NY; Rocky Mount, NC;
      Jacksonville, FL;
Fort Worth, TX; and Memphis, TN.
we be chatting about things that's our business
and sending notes in the section on each other's personalized
      pages
where other folks can leave public comments.

            it's as if the internet is the only safe space for us.

and I feel safer now that I'm living in my tiny room at Ma's town
      house.
UMD accepted all but three of my credits and I start classes in the
      fall.
I've been splitting my days as a marketing intern for a nonprofit
      organization
that serves women victims of domestic violence in PG,
and working in the evenings at Old Navy.
my internship boss Ms. Devereaux is a sweet woman I met at
      GLC

who also sold me my first car "Herbie": a pearl 1988 Audi 90, stick shift.

I'm telling Wesley about Herbie on AIM.

tonydapoet: it feels good to be able to come and go as I please.

bigbrobrodc: I'm glad you finally learned how to prevent from stalling out lol

tonydapoet: hush! it took me some time to figure out how the clutch worked, but I got it now!

bigbrobrodc: well, we both got cars, so perhaps we can meet up soon?

bigbrobrodc: um, hello?

bigbrobrodc: you still there?

tonydapoet: yeah, I'm here. just had to think about it for a second lol

bigbrobrodc: what's there to think about?

tonydapoet: um, I don't even know where to go or what we'd even do.

bigbrobrodc: baby steps, Tony lol. how about we get something to eat and just see how it goes?

tonydapoet: now that sounds like a plan.

I'M NOT AS NERVOUS AS I THOUGHT.

Wesley feels so familiar when we chat online,
but I am curious to see him in the flesh.
and because I'm grown, I don't have to tell Ma where I'm going.
                                    I am officially choosing myself.

I decide to wear my staple uniform and spray Polo Sport cologne
    on my wrist
and rub my hands behind my ears and on my neck.
I check myself in the rearview mirror
and despite the fading dark spots on my cheeks and forehead
my haircut is fresh, my smile is clean, my eyes are clear,
I look cute and I smell good as shit.

we agree to meet at the Applebee's in Largo, MD,
and Wesley smiles as hard as I do when I walk into the restaurant.
somehow, I know to look exactly in his direction.
                                    I guess my gaydar works.
he is seated down at a booth in the corner.
his black curly hair is cut into a fresh low fade, with extra crispy
    edges, like I like mine,
and he's rocking a little part on the side as a special piece of flare.
his roasted chocolate skin is smooth as softened butter

and his eyes are some color stuck between onyx, ebony, and
    mahogany.

he waves his arms high in the air,
I walk over to him casually, trying to avoid looking too pressed.
"are you Tony?" he says, with a voice deeper than I expected.
it's heavy, like he's been storing bass in there his whole life.
    it radiates right through me and I feel like dancing.

we hug, real easy, as if there is no need for physical barrier
    between us,
        and it feels warm and comfortable.
        I ain't never hugged another man without doing the platonic
            bromance dance before.
        it's really nice to feel Wesley's body pressed against mine.

we spend an hour and a half talking about what it's like to finally
    meet each other,
and how I ain't the first person he's met online.
    how he's had some disastrous moments.
        how some folks only wanted to have sex.
            how some folks' hygiene wasn't up to his standard.
it's different hearing Wesley talk the words that I'm used to
    reading.
he tells me I'm twink-size and that he's built average.
I tell him that he's handsome and that he smells good.
we blink at each other a few times
and our knees knock under the table   sometimes by accident.

he asks me if I am comfortable being in public with him.
I tell him I am and that I'd like to do it again.

we split the check for his turkey burger and a side salad
and my bacon cheeseburger and fries, but he pays the tip in cash.

Wesley asks if he can walk me to my car.
    it's dark, but I ain't scared to take a few steps across the
        parking lot.
he is charming, so I don't protest.

we slow stroll to my door and before Herbie opens up,
a rainstorm comes completely out of nowhere
and starts pouring gallons of water from the sky.

it looked like the scene at the end of *Love Jones*
when Darius Lovehall and Nina Mosley were caught in all that
    rain
after she spit that poem onstage about remembering their love,
and Darius tells Nina that he loves her
and that's important like a motherfucker.
and Lauryn Hill said, sometimes you gotta put
                              a mu'fuckah on the end
                          for da ignant niggas to hear.

I am clear that this is the moment Kyle was talking about,
when I will answer my question.

I unlock the passenger door so that Wesley can get in,
the top of his curly head is soaked wet
and the back of his polo shirt is sopping.
I hop in, too, and toss my drenched denim jacket in the back seat.

I turn on the defroster and things are definitely getting steamy.

me and Wesley ain't wasting this divine opportunity,
and I kiss him in my car tonight,
with the thundering and lightning making all that fuss
while we make electricity.

we stay there holding hands, kissing, and laughing and kissing
    some more.
and I discover what that smell I'd been after since being with
    Darin in the closet
tasted like.

I look at myself in the rearview mirror and instead of seeing the
    Boogeyman,
I see a young Black man with knowledge of himself,
who, in the image of God, looks like love.

FALL 2000

THE ONLY THING IS

I can't even think of what words I'd use to tell Ma and Pop their
    only son is gay.
or what language to explain to Tamu why her little brother is
    kissing boys in cars.
I think Ebby knows, or maybe she don't.
I can't tell Blu for obvious reasons, plus we ain't speaking.
and I've distanced myself too far from Bubba's and Cubby's loving
    nicknames
to tell them anything like *this*.

I don't want anyone to know about me and Wesley.
I don't discuss my gigantic secret that I'm truly happy about.
I just swallow down my balloon full of joy
and wait for it to burst butterflies inside my belly that beg me to
    burp,
but I don't because I'm afraid if they escape out of my mouth
they will land in the hands of people who want to push and punch
    me
with their fists, and biblical scriptures, and scripts about
    straightness.

and me and Wesley ain't been past second base,
although he's been hinting that he's eager to catch what I'm
   pitching
and I keep telling him all that getting busy talk is very tempting
but I'm still going to bat in the first inning.
after all, this is just the beginning of what I guess is all my
   sinning.
he's my boy-friend, but I don't think he's my boyfriend.
maybe Wesley is just like Joe was to Uncle UT, my "friend."

I know God been watching all this go down too.
and so far, my fire ain't coming from no pit of Hell,
it's been burning in me since I came out as a shooting star,
so I guess He's waiting to see if I'mma cool myself down or
   something.

I wonder if I'm saved.
If I'm going to heaven.
If I'm a Christian.

And I'm thinking about all these things in my Intro to Psychology
   class,
as our professor is saying something about hearing utterances
of thoughts not belonging to yourself
has been, and is, classified by psychologists as an abnormal
   disease.
I write, "spiritual schizophrenia" at the top of my paper,
close my blue spiral notebook and head to Nyumburu.

I stop in here regularly because I know there is always something
    going on.
last week they sponsored an event between the African Student
    Association and the Latino Student Association called "Taste
    of the Diaspora"
with all this free food, and I'm talking about curry chicken, rice
    and peas,
jollof rice, collard greens, macaroni and cheese, fried plantains,
mofongo, jerk pork, injera and samosas, pupusas,
and doubles with pepper and tamarind sauce.

I walk in and pick up a copy of the *Black Explosion* newspaper;
it has a tagline that says, "presenting the Black community in its
    true light since 1967."
I turn to the third page and see Tiffy's name listed as production
    manager.
I can't wait to tell her how proud I am, but stop in to see Kai and
    Dean first,
the assistant directors of Nyumburu who I met at new student
    orientation.
    they're real cool, relatable administrators who don't
        intimidate students.
    they look like us and I think they're only a few years older
        than me.

Dean is sitting on the radiator in Kai's office
and they appear to be in a heated debate about something.
Kai has hair cornrowed, hanging a little past her shoulders,

and wearing a pair of slim fitted denim jeans, camel brown leather
    boots,
a matching jacket, with a white T-shirt underneath that has
"Hip-Hop Saved My Life" screen-printed on the front.

Dean is a super bright-skinned giant with hazel eyes, and he's
    wearing
a blue NY fitted baseball cap, extra baggy light blue jeans,
a long, short-sleeved striped polo T-shirt with the top buttoned all
    the way up,
and a gold chain layered underneath the collar.

Kai goes, "so, I'm telling the department chair that these students
don't want no fruit and veggie trays at our event,
they want *real* food that reminds them of their cultural homes!"
"oh my bad, I ain't mean to interrupt," I say.
Dean sees me walk in and says, "naw, you're good. wassup, Tony?
that's a nice book bag, homie!"
"thanks man, it's just a little something something," I say,
    pretending to perform vanity.
                With my work-study job in the campus Ombud's office
                and evening shifts at a liquor store across the street from
                                Ma's town house,
                where I make deli sandwiches, punch lotto tickets,
                                and run the cash register,
                I've upgraded my wardrobe to include a brown leather
                                Kenneth Cole satchel
                        that is more about style than function,
                because my books are far too heavy to hold in there.

He goes, "must be nice to be ballin' in college!"
I ain't got no money for real for real, but Dean be tryna gas me up,
so I just roll my eyes and laugh hard at him.

"hey Tony!" Kai says with a gigantic smile.
"if you're looking for Tiffy, she's downstairs."
"okay, thanks!"
"you got your poem ready for the next Juke Joint open mic?" she
    asks.
"you know it's only a few days away, right?"

I think about spiritual schizophrenia and say,
"yeah, I just started working on something as a matter of fact,
but it's far from ready."

Dean goes, "oh, but word on da street is, you got all bars,
so how hard can it be to write one simple poem?"
        if only he *really* knew what all goes down when I write poetry.
                all the listening I be doing to the voice in my head
                        telling me what to write down
                        and how the rhythm and rhyme
                    just find their own place, in their own time.
I quote Erykah Badu, and go,
"Dean, keep in mind I'm an artist, so I'm sensitive about my shit."
we all laugh and I make my way to the *Black Explosion* office.

I GOTTA BE HONEST.

I want to tell Tiffy that I did something with a boy for the first
   time
and I intend to keep on doing things with boys for as long as
   forever is forever
but I can't come out, at least not yet, and certainly not now.
Today, we're celebrating her new role as production manager.

"so, how does it feel to see your name on the page like that?" I ask
   her.
"you already know how much I love reading books and writing
   stories,
but I dream about publishing my own magazine."
she looks over at Jazz, the editor in chief, and says, "I'm grateful
   for you, girl."

Jazz has short brown dreads, sandy skin, and her eyes are either
   chocolate or violet.
She goes, "Tiffy, you were the top candidate, so please, give
   yourself some credit.
I'm just glad you agreed to lug all these papers around campus.
It's fucked up we don't get the same distribution as the

Diamondback,

Black folks' issues matter beyond news praising our star Black
  athletes."

I say, "I know, right?
they still haven't charged the officer who killed my friend Gary."
Jazz goes, "damn shame, bless up brother Gary."
she closes her eyes, puts a peace sign in the air and says,
"one time for the ancestors, ya'll."
Tiffy and I go, "Asé."

                              I love that I can be Black at a PWI.

"Tony, can you drive me around and help put out copies of this
  issue?
I'll pay you back in meal points," Tiffy says with her bright smile.
"you're speaking my love language, of course!"

Jazz goes, "Tiffy tells me that you write poetry, Tony,
so I hope you'll be contributing something to the Poetry Page in
  our next issue."
I go, "I'm still working on something to perform at the Juke Joint."
"perfect, we can publish that poem," Tiffy says, followed by
  "what's it about?"
"um, spiritual schizophrenia," I say.

    I can already tell by their silence that I'm doing that thing
  where my personal poems become cryptic metaphors that only
                              I can crack.

Jazz goes, "that sounds really heavy, you got anything lighter?
like, what was the very first poem you wrote?"
"um, I was in third grade, and it was about changing of the
    seasons."
"there you go, write a poem about the seasons, and we'll publish
    that."

"seasons, huh?" I say, and I feel the solar system spit something out
that's making a beeline for my forehead.

"yeah, seasons, can't they be spiritual things too?" Jazz asks.
                    whole time, Pop been telling me that things happen
                            for a reason and a season.

this poem is coming in hot and fast.
it's all I can think about until I get back home,
pull my notebook out and cross out all parts of spiritual
    schizophrenia
and made a landing strip just a few lines down,
within seconds before the poem smashed into bits
rolling over the paper, drawing lines in the sand, and scratching
    over letters.

I'M GETTING ON THE MIC.

tonight is the Juke Joint and I've been looking forward to this
    event because
of the way Kai hyped it up when I stopped in her office the other
    day.
she said that the concept came from her childhood growing up in
    South Carolina,
and that there were these small and modest community spaces
that came to life on Friday and Saturday nights.
she says the juke joints offered those who worked the hardest,
were paid the least, and struggled on a daily basis
an opportunity to simply laugh, talk, and have a good time, to
    release.

Kai and Dean created a window counter called Otis's Fish Shack,
named after NCC's first director, that is feeding us free fried fish,
hush puppies, red beans and rice, collard greens, and cornbread.
the line to get inside was wrapped around the back of the building.
DJ Oz is up in his booth spinning '90s rap, R&B,
reggae, soul, funk, and go-go music.

I sit with Tiffy, Kelly, and Errica, and see a bunch of my new campus friends are here:

    Jay, a poet, and a sixteen-year-old first-year student who is
        making it cool for

    Black boys to wear colorful crochet kufis on campus.

    Wally, with perfectly twisted long locs who I don't think
        actually goes here.

    Griffin, a painter, and a white boy with red hair who we
        all know is da homie.

    Jessica, the culture creator from Baltimore and future
        UMD NAACP chapter president.

    Mike, the youth preacher who's starting up a Greek-
        lettered organization for Christians.

    Aaron, the spiritual comedian who also got a fancifully
        funny way with words.

    Nicky, the thick sista from the Bronx, who brings me
        sweet treats to class.

Kai settles the room with some call and response, "welcome to
    Juke Joint!"
we all erupt in screams and claps and snaps and applause.
"if y'all ready for your first poet, let me hear you say 'yeah.'"
we all say, "yeah!"
"okay, so up first is a brother who I see on campus almost every
    day,
in fact, I think he might live in Nyumburu somewhere."
Tiffy, Kelli, and I laugh hard enough to snort.
"everyone, please give it up for Tony Keith."

the mic feels good *this* close to my face
and I love looking out at the audience,
knowing that we all are here to have a good time,
be our authentic selves, be seen, be heard, be loved.

I say, "I wrote my first poem in third grade
and it was about the changing seasons.
like many of you, I'm someone whose world is constantly
    changing,
there's always some kind of shift occurring in my universe,
and my father always says, 'everything happens for a reason and a
    season.'

"well, here I am, at nineteen years old,
as the first person in my family to attend college,
and my journey to get here is one that I hope to tell in a book
    someday.
I got some wild-ass stories.

"I've been writing this poem for a little while now
and am going to try to do the whole thing from memory.
ya'll take it easy on me, cool?"
Wally yells out, "alright! alright! alright!"
Jay goes, "let's gooooo, Tonnnnnn!"
Tiff says, "aw, you're gonna have your Darius Lovehall moment."
I close my eyes, inhale, exhale, open them up and from memory, I
    go:

SEASONS

walking atop the earth and ground
and feeling the life in all that surrounds
ain't really nothing new,
I've recognized myself in my world
as early as the age of two
but what my little mind couldn't fathom,
let alone understand,
is that the land I stand on and the air I breathe
wasn't created by "man"

which means man cannot predict
when ice and fire will free-fall from the sky
man cannot manipulate the seasons,
and here's why:

seasons are spiritual entities
supernatural creations,
often confused with "mother nature,"
and it *was* man who created her,
but I'm talking about those seasons
when you've been up too late

worrying about your father's fate
as you hear him regurgitate fluids
consumed with bodily cancer
and that answer
you couldn't figure out on that test
because it's the portion of the material
you missed, on the day you buried your mother
and when your little brother
looks up to you, begging and borrowing
for money to eat lunch after school
and so, you give him your last dollar
because you know he can't be a scholar
if his funds are delinquent

and so the money you spend
is the amount you can't save to buy yourself a car,
because you're tired of catching the morning bus
and hearing people fuss and cuss and gossip
about you, and everything that you do
with "such-and-such" and with "you know who"
and now ya'll having babies
word is, it's twins
and those moments
make you sink instead of swim
that's a season . . .

and I've definitely been through mine
but I've learned in time,

we all get set up, for a comeback

like the moment when you will realize
that your mother left you a check
despite her demise,
so, you can spot your little brother a five
and pay the balance on your tuition bill
and you figure that while your father is still ill
you can drive his truck to get to class,
plus, it's an '88 blue Bronco
and you begin to think
that both "Bronco" and "blue" begin with "B"
and not "C" or "D,"
and "A" was out anyway,
so, the next time you take that test
you circle B as your best guess
and you get it correct
and so the best part about your season,
is that it is over . . .

there's a great deal for us to endure,
but there is no man-made cure
it's only just a season . . .

Spiritual Schizophrenia

~~Hearing utterances of thoughts not belonging to yourself, has been and is classified by psychotherapist as this abnormal disease, a~~

Walking atop the earth and grand and ~~live~~ breathing inside everything that surrounds doesn't strike me as anything "new". I mean I've noticed it all since I was about two, yet what my little mind could not fathom, let alone understand, is that the earth I ~~walk~~ walk upon and this air I breath, wasn't created by man . . . ~~better yet when lst and day the~~ ~~And this man is a push. And with that~~ And that means that man, can't control the seasons. He ~~can't can~~ can't make ~~raise the obate sun rise and he can't or~~ ~~set the sun, stop, no one can~~ the rain stop, he can't ~~put the clouds~~ remove the ice from the sky, man can not change the seasons and I'ma tell you why. Seasons ~~are~~ ~~spiritual beings~~ are spiritual entities confused

supernatural creations, ~~an often interchange~~
w/ Mother Nature, and that was man
that created her, but I'm talking about
a season. and for example those times when
you can't concentrate on ~~your head~~ in yar class
cuz ya were up to late worrying about yar
~~Fate~~ ~~loss~~ fate as yair heard him regurgitate
fluids consumed in bodily cancer, and that
answer ya cold not get when ya took
that test, because thats the portion ~~is~~
of the material ya missed the day ~~yours~~
buried yair mother. And yair brother is
~~dead~~ looking up to ~~feed~~ ya to take care of
him too, ~~and~~ cuz he needs money ~~for school~~
~~since ever~~ to eat lunch at school, and ~~your~~ that
made yar tuition shy a dollar and ya can't
be a scholar if yair funds are delinquent.
~~And that will stop yar academic career and~~
~~you just to choose feel overwhelmed w/~~
~~pressure from your besides like that~~ And
~~that means finding a job, but~~ So next
semester ya wont be able to by that car ~~that~~
that was supposed to be taking yar to school
~~and~~ in the first place, because ya got tired
of taking the bus and ~~here you~~ hearing
the morning cuss and gossip, some

was even about you, and what you was supposed to do with such and such and now you got the virus, and someones having a baby, no twins...!

And those events begin to hurt you within? That is a season, and I've definitly been through mine, but I've learned in time that you get set back, to be set up. So now you realize that ~~the~~ your mom left you ~~some such~~ a check after her demise and ~~you use this and n~~ ya spot your brother five and pay ~~by~~ the balance on ya school bill, and while your pops is still ill, you can use ~~his~~ ~~new blue honda~~ his car to get to class, ~~cor~~ and not to mention its a 98 ~~hyundai accessoire, and~~ ~~your thinking Accessoire Ae~~ Blue Bronco, and you think ~~Bronco~~ Bronco and Blue both begin with ~~be of~~ B, ~~and~~ **But** not C and D and A was out anyway so you ~~get four~~ **circles and** question ~~is~~ correct on your ~~next~~ test, and the best ~~part~~ thing about your season is that ~~there~~ it is ~~over~~ that it is ~~probably~~ over. Somethings are meant for use to endure, and there is no man-made cure.

EPILOGUE

AWAKE AND AWESOME

we fear what we love.
being awesome is a monster trapped inside of closets,
watching us sleep,
stealing our dreams in the dark,
and when we awake,
we forget how amazing we could be,
if we just turned the lights on.

if we just pulled the cover from over our eyes,
placed our feet on the ground,
and boldly proclaimed that we are not afraid of greatness.
that no matter how many nights we shiver, scared of our own
    success,
we will at some point get a full night's rest,
and we will rise with the sun.

and like the sun, we will be bright
and blinding and bold and hot and huge,
and people will need *us*
to survive the cold and the night.

and we will awaken as warriors of weary.

as soldiers of failure.

as griots of fate.

armed with weapons of mass construction,

we will build ourselves a fortress of power,

protecting ourselves from hating to be loved,

and our capacity to be God-like.

and our right to be present.

and our calling to parents to offspring of our victories,

and ancestors to heartache, and loneliness and confusion,

and empty pockets, and grumbling bellies.

and we will awaken, with muscles up on our shoulders

that are strong enough to hold the world up,

when people need us to hold the world up,

because they're tired of holding the world up.

and we will awaken, with our voices in harmony and pitch,

that makes a WHISPER seem like a rocket ship,

and a rocket ship sound like "I miss you."

and we will tiptoe down hallways

making footprints feel like earthquakes.

and we will awaken all those who are sleeping,

all those afraid to be brilliant,

all those afraid to be acknowledged for daring to be different.

for those who run, when they should stand.

for those who hush, when then they should command.

for those who need to realize you cannot hide in the light.
it sticks to you like brown does on my Black skin.
like sap from trees, rooted in sweet soil.

you need to see that you are a star.

I literally see YOU in the sky.
defying laws of space, time, and gravity,
because humans are not supposed to fly,
but you glide like the first leaf in autumn.
your silhouette struts in daylight
and dances with the moon.

you are part of a collective.
a critical mass of intellectuals governed by divine knowledge.
which means you are meant to be here with purpose.
just like I am meant to be here with purpose.
we are all purposefully meant to be here,

so that the sick can become a healer.
so that the timid can become a leader.
so that the weary can become a teacher.
and so that the Boogeyman could become a poet.

ACKNOWLEDGMENTS

I am grateful for my ancestors, who I know be watching. Hubs, I love you real hard. My entire family and all my dearest friends, I am because you are. Shout-out to my publishing "dream team;" y'all get me. Ed Emcee Academy squad, I appreciate all the gas whenever I was writing this book while running on fumes. Jay—my brother, you are a pillar. Mama, I made it.